The Spirit of Smiling:

Perfecting the Art of Surrendering to The Way

Gary Giamboi

Here's what the Experts' reviews have to say about

The Spirit of Smiling:
Perfecting the Art of Surrendering to The Way

Book Review:

The Spirit of Smiling: Perfecting the Art of Surrendering to The Way is a beautiful, inspiring guidebook in which author Gary Giamboi takes us step by step to a journey towards enlightenment.

The relevant anecdotes and logical explanations on truth blended with profound teachings make it easy and useful for a sincere seeker on the path of truth. An analytical approach covering many aspects of life in defining the obstacles and simple solutions to reach the highest goal makes the book more appealing.

The chapter on free will gives a clear understanding of choice a human being is gifted with by God in the following concept:

"As long as we are pursuing something we desire to make ourselves happy, we are not using our free will."

"It is in our human nature to want pleasure and avoid pain. Choosing actions which achieve these ends is like water flowing downhill. By using free will to rise above our human nature and acting like a being on a higher plane, we are actually working on giving up our free will and assuming the nature of a being on a higher plane."

Finally, the author has put the essence of the book in this quote: "Our life's true and only purpose is to regain control of our true selves. And like it or not, change is the only way to do it."

I am sure this book will help the readers to clarify their doubts and bring new inspiration in their lives.

— *Swami Atmavidyananda Giri*
Vice President at Kriya Yoga Institute, http://www.kriya.org/
"That is the path which is directed by the realized."
"Meditate and be realized."
Swami Atmavidyananda Giri is a senior monk in the lineage of Paramahamsa Hariharananda and Paramahamsa Prajnanananda. He is currently Vice president of the Kriya Yoga Institute

The Spirit of Smiling by Gary Giamboi

Gary Giamboi has cleverly pulled up a meditation cushion and invited us to join him on a very intimate and personal talk on the path to enlightenment. Hidden in plain sight amongst the simplicity of uncomplicated words and examples from everyday experiences lies the gift of someone who has spent years dedicated to the search for Truth. Pour yourself a cup of tea, settle into yourself and enjoy a one-on-one session with your personal guru.

The Spirit of Smiling reveals how years of discipline in martial arts can be the key to mastering the biggest enemy any person will ever have- themselves. There is no need to read hundreds of pages to understand what is so plainly stated in this book. Shifu Gary chooses a simple language that anyone can understand and avoids the flowery words or smoke & mirrors that ego-centered writers often choose to boost their appearance.

This is a practical book, a "get to the point" opportunity for someone who is committed to self-improvement.

Of special interest to seekers and teachers, is Chapter 2 which expertly defines the responsibility of both student and teacher. It calls forth the subject of accountability within the student that is so often overlooked by newcomers on the journey. It is an essential first step to clarify the dynamic at play in the process of enlightenment. That it is not something that can be bestowed upon a seeker, but a conscious process of personal integration.

The Spirit of Smiling continues to describe point by point the typical places we stumble on in the process of purification while at the same time reassuring us that it is normal, expected and nothing to be afraid of. Shifu Gary takes philosophical ideas like wuwei (the term for non-action in Daoism) and, without ever mentioning the words, effortlessly guides us into understanding its essence.

Step by step he describes the process of liberation ultimately guiding us into a state of pure bliss where the most natural thing occurs, a smile.

Enjoy!

— Christina J Barea, DP, MMQ
Daoist Priest, Qigong Therapist & Instructor
www.TheRisingLotus.com
Author of "Qigong Illustrated"

The Spirit of Smiling by Gary Giamboi

"Gary imparts knowledge distilled from his years of both his life experience and his studying Eastern spiritual practices.

In this book you will find explanations of Eternal Wisdom in everyday understandable language. Difficult concepts are explained with wonderful stories and metaphors which make essential points easy to relate to.

This exceptional book is truly a treasure and one to refer to again and again.

The writing style is such that the reader is engaged in a conversation with the author. This reader's experience felt as if Gary was speaking directly to her and during the process of reading, a True Smile appeared on her face. "

— Suzanne Stier, PhD
Consultant to Family Owned Businesses and Religious Institutions
Certified Spiritual Director

In *The Spirit of Smiling,* Gary Giamboi draws on the principles of various Eastern traditions including Vedanta, Buddhism, and Daoism as he critically examines various topics including the process of teaching and learning, the cultivation of wisdom, and transcending the ego.

Lucid and clearly written, Giamboi applies Asian theories of emptiness, karma, non-duality, and self-hood to everyday situations and circumstances confronting Western audiences.

The Spirit of Smiling is an excellent primer for lay audiences wishing to study how Eastern philosophy may be practically applied in modern times. Each chapter of this text may be read individually for points to meditate upon. The book as a whole, however, takes the reader through a self-reflective journey in which we meditate upon the simple but profoundly significant act of smiling.

— *Rohit Singh*
PhD Candidate, Department of Religious Studies

UC Santa Barbara

The Spirit of Smiling:
Perfecting the Art of Surrendering to The Way

Copyright © 2012 by The Institute of Asian Arts, LLC. All rights reserved. No portion of this book, except for brief reviews, may be reproduced in any form without the written permission of The Institute of Asian Arts, LLC.

Cover Design by Ashe Higgs

For information, contact The Institute of Asian Arts, LLC at
www.TheInstituteofAsianArts.com
@DharmaWarrior

ISBN: 061565925X
ISBN-13: 9780615659251

Contents

1. Dedication xv
2. Foreword. 1
3. Preface 5
4. The Processes of Teaching and Learning 17
5. The Village Monk. 29
6. Knowledge vs. Intelligence vs. Wisdom. 31
7. A "Few" Words About Enlightenment 37
8. Polishing One's Mirror 41
9. Simple is Good, or Is It?. 49
10. What Really Gets Tired?. 55
11. Thinking vs. Doing vs. Being. 59
12. The Process of Smiling 69
13. How About A Little Magic? 73
14. How Many Different People Are There? 81
15. The Process of Letting Things Come to Us 87
16. What if We Got What We Wanted? 97
17. To Change or Not To Change 101
18. Moving Beyond Our Egos 109
19. A Little Bit About Free Will. 120
20. The Monk and the Highwayman 127
21. Would You Like Some Bliss? 131
22. When Is Our Free Will Truly Free?. 137
23. The Big Problem With Mindfulness: How Do We Use the Information Stored in Our Memories Without Living in the Past?. 149
24. Two Traveling Monks 153
25. One Last Question 157
26. In Conclusion. 163
27. About the Author. 165

Dedication

This book is dedicated to Everything that has lead up to This moment.

Every morning, I begin my day by offering my most profound gratitude to All of my instructors for the help they have given to me. Without their help, I would not be as I am now nor as I will be in the next moment.

I am very grateful to my lovely and loving wife, Lisa, who stuck with me as our lives changed; and helped me get through some very tough times.

I believe I owe much of my present State of Being to her nurturing of me.

She has taken the art of Lacto-Vegetarian cooking to such lofty heights that all of my carnivorous friends are jealous of my diet.

I am also grateful to my parents and all of the wonderful people I have met along the way for just being themselves and letting me touch their lives as they have touched mine.

To all of you, I give my Blessing:

Dhanyavad!

("May All Blessings Be for You; May All Goodness Go to You.")

— *Gary Giamboi, aka, Gajendranathan*

Foreword

An Energetic Renaissance is underway. A deep spiritual need is awakening as people are becoming increasingly more aware of the fact something is 'missing' in their lives.

Standard conventions and institutions are in a state of decline as people begin coming to terms with the understanding that true health and wellbeing is dependent upon the responsibility one takes for one's self, in every aspect of one's life.

The victim mentality and its aspect of slavery to those things we think or have been told will save us, is falling away. The mantra: *Give me a pill to suppress the symptomology so I can get back to the delusional lifestyle that gave rise to the problem in the first place* - is being seen for the insanity it truly is.

The process of reconnecting with the part of us that has been beaten down through the over-lording of the ego is not an easy one. Years, decades, even generations of conditioning are at play and, in my opinion, are responsible for the decline and emptiness today's society is experiencing.

If you can honestly observe the state of things and people, you can see that all problems emanate from the emptiness of the human spirit/soul brought about by an ego-driven, materially-focused approach to life.

The Spirit of Smiling

Our Inner Voice, which is the direct connection to Divinity however you understand it, has been muffled by the cacophony of how most people have chosen, unconsciously in most cases, to live their lives.

But the voice is still there, and is always speaking to us. All we need to do is learn how to listen to what has always been, and will always be there for us.

So how do we turn it around? How does one stop on a dime and change direction after you've been travelling the same road at 100 miles per hour?

Here's the good news: If you're reading these words you are already aware your life needs changing. To paraphrase the Buddha, *Once the word 'Enlightenment' comes into your life, the outcome is guaranteed.*

But the novice traveler embarking on what to them may be the strange, confusing, and often frustrating path of self-examination and self-cultivation will often seek the guidance of those who have gone before.

Throughout the time humanity has existed, there have always been 'Children of Light' who have walked among us. Christ, Buddha, and countless other Luminous Beings whose message and very presence served to elevate the consciousness and awareness of those who had the good fortune to experience their presence, have always been with us.

Their teachings have served as beacons lighting the way through the darkness for those in whom the Inner Voice awakens. But as one travels the path, one gains the understanding that the pursuit is the reward, and the Light from without, is the same Light that shines from within.

If one mindfully travels the path, step by step, breath by breath, the true understanding of the exquisite nature of, and incomprehensible depth and beauty of the present moment may reveal itself.

The statement *Truth is Exquisitely Simple* can only be fully embraced after many years, if not lifetimes of self-cultivation. Although, if the soil and conditions are right, a seed can germinate and sprout amazingly fast.

Many of us in whom the Inner Voice awakened understand our life-path as a calling. And as Peace and Compassion flood your heart, the natural reaction, at least in my opinion, is to offer assistance to others if they are ready to begin their journey.

Enter Gary Giamboi.

Gary and I currently serve on the Board of Directors of the National Qigong Association (NQA) and it is through that organization we met.

What immediately struck me about Gary was, what was later confirmed for me by his impressive accomplishments, a depth, pureness, and simplicity of character.

Gary 'sees it.'

The Spirit of Smiling

I was truly honored when he asked me to write this foreword for, what I hope will be a series of his works.

To be able to convey concepts and thought processes succinctly and logically while expressing the true simplicity at the heart of the matter takes a depth of understanding many aspire toward.

Gary has obviously devoted his life and energies to traveling the path and now seeks to do, what I feel is the next logical step in the process: share his work in the hope it may help spread the light and understanding which lies in the heart of us all.

To those travelers who have begun the journey: Embrace the vehicle; but remember the purpose of a vehicle is to transport you somewhere. Don't forget to get out of the vehicle every now and again and enjoy the landscape. I think Alan Watts said it best, "You can't get wet from the word water."

Thanks Gary!

— *Mark R. Reinhart*

馬 克 永 學 ▨ 三 清 河 道

Mark R. Reinhart is the president of the National Qigong Association (2011-2013).

Preface

Let me begin by explaining my personal style of writing.

The first issue I must tell you about is my choice of gender specific pronouns when their antecedent can be either gender.

Hopefully, this will be my book's most inexact subject.

I have no personal agenda to promote on this issue.

I actually wrote this book using the *he/she* variant; and, when the book was finished and I read it through, I hated the way this compromise made my book read.

I then re-edited the book using only the masculine pronouns when referring to a gender neutral antecedent.

The English language needs a neutral gender pronoun.

Until it has one, writers will be forced to choose between having their work read well or politically correctly.

The inability to use this much needed pronoun was especially burdensome to me because I believe The Supreme Entity is gender neutral.

This issue is a clearly defined problem with a solution I am not comfortable with.

The rest of the issues concerning my writing style cannot be clearly defined; but I am totally comfortable with my solutions. I hope you will be too.

Most people know the vast majority of the meanings we perceive from a conversation are derived from the speaker's tone of voice, oral inflections, the timing and phrasing of the words, as well as, the facial expressions and body language of the speaker.

The precise literal meanings of the spoken words supply us with a much smaller amount of our total understanding of what is being communicated to us.

Unfortunately, this book will give you access only to my written words. Therefore, in order to facilitate you understanding more of what I am trying to "say" using only the words in this book, I have attempted to write this book for you in manner which more closely resembles my speaking directly to you.

I tried to be less formal, more personal and, most importantly, more cognizant of the fact that if I can make myself accessible to you as a real person through my personal style of writing, you will be better able to follow my train of thought.

This was not meant to pre-dispose you into agreeing with me by making me seem to be a nice guy. It was done solely to help you understand why and how I see things as I do. I tried my best to leave it up to you to draw your own conclusions about what I have written or should that be "what I have said" in this book.

You will notice I seem to capitalize words in a random manner. However, let me assure you it is not random. Long before email came into existence, I began to spell the words I wished to emphasize the importance of with capital letters.

I use capitalization to try to reflect how the tone and inflection of my voice would change just as if I was speaking to you.

So kindly be guided accordingly.

I wrote this book to share with you some of the insights I have had while traveling my path. I have included numerous teaching stories drawn from several ancient traditions which illustrate some of the points I am "talking" to you about.

You may have read some or even all of them before. And although I like to re-read them every now and then, my main purpose in including them is to show you that I did not make this stuff up!

I am merely presenting The Truths in a more detailed way than these old stories do.

I have studied many traditions (kindly refer to the *About the Author* section at the end of this book) which on the surface may seem very different to each other.

However, let me say loud and clear: I perceive All I have studied to be much more similar than not.

This point of view has served me very well.

It is because I have come to realize:

"Things are Only One Way."

Even though we may not understand what That Way is or even see It, Everything has only One True Essence, One True Nature.

Actually, it is our "job" to Realize This, Accept This and Unify with This.

This book is the first in a series of books in which I will try to cut through many of the nebulous concepts associated with the traditions that deal with the spiritual and energetic planes of existence.

Specifically, we will look at how surrendering or letting go is absolutely essential to seeing, reaching and living on the Higher Spiritual and Emotional Planes of Existence.

Letting go of your ego is much more difficult than denying its existence, selectively denying parts of it or just simply beating it into submission. Yet, letting go of your ego is the only way to truly change yourself.

For example, let's look at one of the most common changes people try to make to themselves: Losing Weight.

The reason most weight loss programs and diets ultimately fail is they are designed merely to entice a person to change their behavior solely to reach their desired goal.

These diets would work much better in the long term if they changed their focus from this short term result to changing that part of the dieter from which the desires that lead to over eating originate from.

Why?

Because that behavior originates in what makes that person who and what they actually are. Therefore, changing this part of themselves would be tantamount to changing themselves as they perceive themselves to be.

Even though changing themselves is the surest way of changing their behavior, most people do not want any part of this process.

It can be very scary for most of us; unless you truly believe you have nothing of real value to lose in the process.

However, since losing certain parts of ourselves is the point of this book, I'll save the rest of this particular discussion for later.

Therefore, let's return to my previous point about what happens when we try to change our behavior by starting a diet without changing the part of ourselves that actually gives rise to that particular behavior.

When someone forces himself to repress the behavioral tendencies which form out of the desires that emanate from his Heart of Hearts, the pressure to manifest these tendencies will continue to grow. This pressure will continue to increase until it is great enough to shatter the cages around those tendencies that were created by his decision to follow the rules of the diet.

These tendencies will then begin to manifest themselves into actions; and thus, that diet is destined to fail as soon as the person's behavior inevitably returns to its "normal" operating mode.

Most of us pursue our spiritual quests in the same manner we pursue our diets.

We force ourselves to adopt certain behavioral modifications in order to achieve the results we are looking for as quickly as possible. We do this without making the effort or taking the time to change our egos and our inner most values which actually dictate the behaviors we choose.

Therefore, most spiritual quests end up exactly as most diets do.

I don't know about you, but I have heard many overweight people say: "I felt so much better when I was keeping my weight down by sticking to my diet. I had more energy, I reduced or eliminated my medicines and I looked much better than I do now."

I have also heard many stressed out, hyper or overly anxious people say: "I felt so much better when I was following my routine and meditating every day. I felt so much more relaxed and calm, and much more peaceful than I do now."

This is how similar both the successes and failures of these two seemingly different programs are.

Short term modifications can work well if they are the correct behavior patterns for the intended goal. However, regardless of the positive results we can achieve in the short term by modifying our behavioral patterns, most of us still find it extremely difficult to go against our inner most values for very long.

The inner discord, stress or unease we feel when our actions conflict with our most important values will almost always, in the long run, outweigh the pleasure we may derive from doing those actions. And, if for some reason, the displeasure doesn't get to us, the amount of energy we have to expend to swim against the current by acting against our own nature will eventually cause us to become too fatigued to continue this battle for very long.

Slowly, but inexorably, our growing fatigue will cause us to lower our battle shield and to swing our sword at the enemy with less and less power. At some point, we will weaken enough to enable our enemy to overcome us easily.

It is obvious to me we would achieve much longer lasting changes to ourselves (perhaps even permanent changes) if we stopped trying to get the results we think we want immediately.

Instead, we should be content with focusing on making the changes we need to make to our inner most values.

You have a much higher chance of successfully completing a journey if, while you are traveling, you are focused on the journey itself; and, not day dreaming about the final destination.

If we are actually successful at making the required changes to ourselves, the goals we thought we wanted would automatically manifest themselves at some point in the future when the conditions became just right for them to appear.

Did you notice I used the phrase "thought we wanted," instead of "wanted." This is because once we make these kinds of changes to our values and to ourselves, our desires have a very good chance of changing also.

Why?

Because as our values change, our desires will then arise from these new values.

The greater the difference is between these new values and the ones they replaced, the greater the difference will be between our new desires and our former desires.

I know this is a tough way to go for someone who lives in a society which is doing its best to eliminate the time between the rise of a desire and its seeming fulfillment. Indeed, our society is not only trying to completely eliminate this time lag, it is actually trying to convince us this is a good thing, this is the way things should be and we have a right to the instant gratification of our desires.

But, just as fruit left to ripen on the vine will always taste sweeter than fruit that was picked too early simply to satisfy our desire to have it now, a change initiated in ourselves will always bear sweeter fruit if it is left to develop and manifest in its own time, according to its own nature.

Therefore, let's focus on taking as much time as we need to concentrate our efforts on changing that part of ourselves which governs our core values. These are the values which dictate which decisions we make, why we make them and even exactly when we make them.

If we did change that part of ourselves which governs our core values, then the behavioral changes we seek would eventually manifest themselves automatically, of their own volition and in their own time.

This process is truly simple.

Unfortunately, without guidance and perseverance, it can also be very difficult for most of us.

The Spirit of Smiling

One of my duties is to do my best to help my personal students learn Martial Arts, Yoga, Qigong and several other Eastern Disciplines that they wish me to help them learn.

In so doing, I point out to all of them over and over again I spend more time telling them what not to do, what to stop doing and what to let go of than in giving them "new" actions or "new" things to learn.

It is hard for most people to accept the fact that performing an action with corrections Is performing a New action.

One of my favorite quotes is from Zen Buddhism: "Boredom is a Lack of Paying Attention to Detail."

Given enough attention to detail or focus, Everything is constantly new.

The surface of a glass of water is not very exciting to look at. However, put a drop of that water under a microscope and a whole universe of activity is there to catch and keep your attention from wandering.

The same is true of our lives.

The closer you pay attention to Everything you do, the less your mind will become bored with Everything you do.

I hope this book will help you understand people are usually their own greatest obstacle to learning and progressing.

The more things you possess, the greater the probability that not only will one of them get in your way at any given point in space and time; but, that the one that does get in your way will be the one you can't get around, over or through.

We can make our job much more difficult than it needs to be by over complicating things.

I believe many teachers are also guilty of this.

When faced with the task of trying to explain something which cannot be explained in words by using words, these teachers insist on trying to accomplish the impossible. They end up using far too many words and comparative concepts because they do not know how to explain in words something they, themselves, do not truly understand in words.

One of the things we all know how to do, but we can't put into words is the Process of Smiling.

Somehow, One Thing we seem to almost Always get Right is a Smile.

This book will look at the Process of Smiling.

In so doing, I will attempt to show you how you can expand on this process in order enable yourself to use that exact same process as often as possible to manifest what makes you what everyone should be attempting to become: Enlightened.

The Processes of Teaching and Learning

The Buddha said:

*"It is You that must do The Work.
Masters only point The Way."*

The first concepts I believe we need to explore and, hopefully, get behind us is: What does it mean "to teach" someone something, what does it mean "to learn" something; and, what are the respective duties of a teacher and a student.

First, Foremost and Last we all need to remember:

No One can "Teach" Anything to Anyone!

Let me repeat this:

You, I and everyone else Cannot be taught Anything by Anyone: not at Any Time, at Any Place or Anyhow.

Don't misunderstand me: Most Certainly, we can learn.

However, "Learn" is an active verb. It is something we, the students, do. "Learn" is a concept that doesn't apply to the teacher.

"Teach" is also an active verb. It is something a teacher does. However, it is a concept that doesn't exist for the student.

A teacher cannot "Learn" something to or for another person.

A teacher cannot teach a student anything if by "teach a student" we mean the student passively "learns" what was being taught by some means other than by the student Realizing it or "Learning" it for himself.

By teaching something well, the teacher can facilitate the student's learning. If the student learns while the teacher is teaching (or while thinking about the teacher's teachings), we can say the teacher facilitated or helped the student's learning.

This is what Teachers are supposed to do. This is what Good Teaching accomplishes.

If a teacher presented the material to his students and no one understood the lesson, did the teacher teach?

I believe he did.

He may or may not have performed his job or duty as a teacher well; but, he did do it.

It all boils down to this:

I disagree with one of the accepted meanings of the verb "teach."

I do agree with a teacher being someone who teaches, as in presents, a subject.

I disagree with the definition of the word "teach" when it means to teach someone, as in, "to give knowledge to."

Why do I disagree with an accepted scholarly definition of this word?

Because I believe the words we use to define a concept will influence how we think about that concept. In this case, the concepts are "the relationship between teaching and learning" and "what are the duties of a teacher and a student."

How a person defines these concepts will determine how much responsibility he will take for the amount, kind and quality of knowledge he acquires; and, how much effort he needs to expend in doing so.

For example: in my opinion, it makes no sense to say the following: "I gave him a gift; but, he refused it."

Instead, we should say: "I offered him a gift; but, he refused it."

In order for one person to give something to someone, it must be taken by the person to whom you are giving it to.

"Offering" is not "giving." "Offering" can be done unilaterally. "Giving" cannot. "Giving" requires "taking," and therefore cannot be accomplished unilaterally.

For the exact same reasons, a teacher can only teach; a student can only learn. These two processes can be connected; but, they are not the same.

In fact, just like "giving" and "taking," they are completely different processes.

Let me ask the question this way:

"If a teacher did a fantastic job of presenting the material and no one understood the lesson, did the teacher teach anything to anyone"?

Do you see how asking this question puts the burden of teaching on the student and of learning on the teacher?

We are judging the quality of the "teaching" solely by the amount of learning that takes place.

If a great chef made a fantastic meal, served and presented it beautifully and no one ate a forkful of this wonderful meal, would anyone question whether or not the chef actually cooked anything that tasted great?

Absolutely not.

Why?

Because no one judges the quantity or even the quality of the cooking by the amount that was eaten. They are not related.

Whether a person eats nothing from a great meal or stuffs himself on terrible food has no bearing on how much food was cooked or how good the food tasted.

However, somehow our society has equated how much was learned with the quantity and the quality of the teaching.

"Teacher" is a terrible word because of this fact.

How can someone be called something that denotes that person does something that cannot be done by that person?

Instead of "teacher," we could say "presenter," facilitator" or "helper," because that is what a "teacher" can do.

He can present a subject or an idea.

The more vivid the description, the more ways of presenting an idea or concept a person has, the greater the chance the "Teacher" has of "helping" another person accept or learn whatever it is the presenter is trying to describe.

Notice I didn't use the word "explain."

This is because you cannot explain something to someone unless they understand what you mean.

As you can see, the problem with the meaning of "explain" is exactly the same as with "teaching."

If you were to read the most widely acclaimed explanation of a subject to someone, and that person does not understand what you are explaining, then you did not explain it to him.

The Spirit of Smiling

Perhaps the following anecdote may seem silly; but, it will make my point:

Suppose you were to bring the most successful and most sought after teacher in all of Japan to the USA, and had him give his most perfectly detailed explanations (in Japanese of course) to an audience which spoke only English.

Do you think he explained his subject well?

Do you think he explained it to anyone?

Do you think anyone learned anything?

Of course he explained everything well.

He just didn't explain Anything to Anyone who was present. And of course, no one learned anything.

Obviously, it would be silly for a teacher to try to teach his students something new while speaking a language the students did not know.

Or is it?

While I do agree if teaching a complete class in a foreign language would make it impossible to learn very much about a new subject, doesn't teaching all new concepts require a student to learn the meanings of new words, new meaning for words already understood in another way or at the very least putting already understood meanings together in a new way?

The best explanations help a person make a connection between the concepts he already understands and the new information which he is attempting to "learn" or assimilate.

For example, the hardest part of learning the concept of numbers is learning the very first number (usually the number "one").

Once a person understands what one number represents, it is much easier for them to build upon their understanding of what that number means to make the leap of understanding to the next number. And so on.

Do you remember a few paragraphs ago in the Preface I wrote "I do my best **to help my personal students learn** Martial Arts, Yoga, Qigong and several other disciplines"

I honestly did not choose that wording because I wanted to refer to that passage here. Those words flowed naturally from my fingertips because I truly believe them.

It is my duty as a teacher to Help my students to do their duty, which is to learn what they need to learn.

This is the reason I didn't say "I teach Martial Arts to my students." I only Help them learn Martial Arts.

There is an old Martial Art's saying:

"When the student is ready, his teacher will appear."

I believe this adage actually means much more than what it seems to imply.

Of course, those of you who know how the ancient sages taught will not be surprised at this.

I translate this adage into "When the student is ready, he will understand; and, not one moment before."

In other words, regardless of what a "teacher" may say or do, the student's understanding and learning will not happen one instant before everything that needs to be in place, is in place and ready to go.

Therefore, when someone, something or some set of circumstances is able to provide a person with the concept(s) he needs in order to make the connection between what he already knows and a new piece of knowledge, then that person, thing or set of circumstances facilitated the learning process.

He or it became the specific teacher needed by that specific person at that specific point in space and time in order to learn that specific piece of knowledge.

This is true whether the "student" wanted to "learn" that information or not; and, also whether or not the "teacher" intended to "teach" that concept or not.

One obvious, but often over looked point, is the greater the desire to learn something is, the more likely something will be learned.

Notice I did not say "the more likely 'It' will be learned." The desire to learn will certainly facilitate learning. However, since you are dealing with the Unknown, the future will be impossible to predict.

Many students blame their lack of understanding and learning on having a poor "teacher."

Obviously, if a teacher doesn't know something, he can't intentionally "teach" it or "present" it to you or "help" you learn it. However, the teacher's deficiencies do not let the student off the hook.

It is the responsibility and the duty of the student to find the right "teacher." The more a student wants to learn something, the easier it will be for him to fulfill this duty.

It does not matter you need the "teacher" because you don't know what you are trying to learn. You need to make it your business to know what you need to know in order to pick the correct "teacher"... at least eventually.

In other words, the teacher you picked when you did not know anything may not be the one you should stay with after you begin to acquire some level of knowledge.

All things must change and evolve.

You may find that just by chance you picked a teacher who was much better than you ever imagined. Or, you may decide your teacher, who up until this moment was terrific for you, is no longer right for you as you are now.

The Spirit of Smiling

The ancient people of the Far East demonstrated their knowledge about the processes of teaching and learning when they picked their words for "teacher."

The Japanese use the word *Sensei*, which means "he who was born before." This implies he has more of the knowledge of what it takes to successfully undertake a certain path or course of action because he has already done it or has done it for a longer period of time.

It is also used in Japan as a term of respect for the knowledge someone has acquired regardless of whether or not they "teach" that knowledge.

In Chinese Martial Arts or Gung Fu, the term *sifu* or *shifu* means Master, as in a Master of an art and not "teacher." It implies a master is needed to help a student along his path, which is the same as the master's was.

The Chinese have a proverb which is based upon the same premise as this chapter: "Teachers open the door, but you must walk through it yourself."

My favorite term to use for "teacher" is the Sanskrit word for teacher, *Guru*. The term *Guru* means "Remover of Darkness." It does not mean Bringer of Light. It does not mean teacher.

Even here, one must remember if someone were to destroy the darkness by removing all the veils covering a person's eyes, that person still has to open his "eyes" and look in the right direction in order to see what there is to see.

In the same way, even if a "Guru" helped opened a person's Third Eye[1], that person would still have work to do in order to understand what there is to understand.

Both the "teacher" and the student have responsibilities.

The student must learn.

The "teacher" should do more than just teach or present.

He must do more than lay the knowledge out in front of the student. A teacher with good intentions will keep repeating the lesson over and over in different ways until one of the ways is the one the student "needs" to hear.

He will watch the student's reaction to a lesson and gauge whether or not it seemed to move the student in the right direction. He will play the game of "getting warmer or colder" with himself in order to keep refining his lessons based upon the student's reactions until he has taken the student as far as he can.

What makes a teacher good instead of merely good intentioned is that the better a teacher is at choosing which concepts to use in attempting to make his point understood, the fewer attempts he will need to accomplish his goal.

---

1 Third Eye: As used here by me, refers to the point where we seem to "see" and understand things with our mind. Many texts place it in the center of the forehead. Thus making the inside of our forehead the rear side of our mental movie screen.

"The Opening of the Third Eye" usually refers to the Power of "seeing" "Things As They Truly Are" or The Truth.

As you can see, I believe the final burden of learning is on the student, even to the point of choosing the right teacher.

Don't be confused with the "more is better" syndrome many in the West suffer from.

"Better" is better, "more" is only more; especially when it comes to choosing the "best" teacher for yourself.

If you found the world's most knowledgeable expert on a subject and he agreed to instruct you, would you think you had found the absolute best teacher for yourself?

What if that person's personality and teaching style was such that, at best, you would only be able to learn half of what he knew?

Let's say a friend of yours found another instructor who knows only seventy percent of what your teacher knows. Eventually, it dawns on you that if you learned under this new teacher, you would be able to learn everything this person knew.

With which teacher would you learn more?

Would the more knowledgeable person be the "better" teacher for you in this instance?

Let me end this discourse on teaching by using an old Chinese tale to illustrate the point about teaching and learning being separate skills.

The Village Monk

There was once monk who lived in a remote village. Its residents were very poor. However, they all loved this monk and his teachings so much, they feed him and gave him a place to sleep in return for his staying with them and teaching them every day.

After many years of teaching the villagers, the monk had accepted a small group of disciples from among them. One day, a disciple came to him and said:

"Sifu," how can you continue to teach these people every day when they have not changed one tiny bit after all of these years'?

The monk replied:

"I see you too have learned nothing after all of these years.

Do you think I teach for them?

I teach because it is My duty to teach.

It is Their duty to learn.

Can I let Their failure to do Their duty stop Me from doing My duty"?

Knowledge vs. Intelligence vs. Wisdom

Another point we should clarify is how I define the differences between Knowledge, Intelligence and Wisdom.

Knowledge is simply acquired facts. It is individual quantum bits of information which have been memorized and categorized.

Knowledge does not have to be understood correctly for the facts to be correct.

Not understanding a piece of knowledge may limit its usefulness; but, it will still be true. Indeed, the Knowledge can be true; but, the Understanding may be incorrect.

Intelligence goes beyond knowledge. Intelligence leads to Understanding. The greater the Intelligence, the more likely the Understanding will be correct.

Understanding an individual piece of Knowledge means you are able to use That Piece of Knowledge in a rational, logical way.

The Understanding of an idea or concept can occur when individual bits of knowledge can be linked to other individual bits of knowledge in a way that enables their information to become conceptualized in some logical way.

This process results in the formation of new knowledge enabling the concept to be put to proper use.

One can then repeat this process by using one's Intelligence again in order to understand the new knowledge. If this process is successful, it can lead to even more New Knowledge.

These new pieces of knowledge gained solely through the process of Understanding can then lead to another new Understanding.

This process is cyclical and is only limited by the intellect or intelligence of the person.

Wisdom, however, is something totally different.

True Wisdom requires Insight and Intuition.

True Wisdom enables new understandings to manifest themselves directly, without the necessity of a conscious, logical, rational thought process as the driving force behind it.

Sometimes, it is not possible acquire certain pieces of Wisdom by thinking only logical, rational thoughts. You may need to make a leap of understanding from point A and get to point C without passing through point B.

Even though overt, scientifically accepted logic may have been missing in the process, True Wisdom must be just as accurate as if all the steps of a scientifically accepted proof were present and accounted for.

Of course, this also happens to be the great problem with True Wisdom. Since it is not arrived at through a step by step process, it is easy to miss the mark and never know it.

This is why there are so many foolish ideas and concepts that refuse to wither and die.

However, if you wish to attain True Wisdom, you must be willing to accept the risks involved with this process.

True Wisdom does not refer to a higher level of processing knowledge or understanding that knowledge in ways no one else has thought of.

True Wisdom refers to being able to put Things in their "Proper Prospective" in The Way Things Truly Are.

People who have shown they can link knowledge together in ways no one else can and thereby generate new understandings are called geniuses. This gift alone will not make a person Wise.

People considered Wise are those who have demonstrated the ability to live their lives in a manner which seems to solve life's difficult problems with the least amount of pain and suffering.

Wise people have the ability to see things clearly. Usually, this is because they do not acknowledge or give credence to the processes which complicate things for most people.

These processes are usually the result of our egos seeking to avoid pain or experience happiness. When this happens, our focus becomes avoiding pain or experiencing happiness instead of dealing with life as we should: Doing our duty (*Dharma* in Yoga) while leaving as small a "Personal Footprint" on the rest of Creation as we can.

If we can accomplish this, then it is much easier to see things clearly and for what they Truly Are.

This clarity enables Wise people to stay focused on what is important. The Solutions to their problems are more obvious to them than to people who are less Wise.

True Wisdom narrows your choices down to one: The Proper One in Accordance With The Way Things Are.

It is difficult to pick the wrong solution when there is Only One Choice!

Unfortunately, although having Wisdom will make it easier for someone to make the correct decision, it may not make living with the correct decision easy.

It may make it easier because you know what you have decided is the Right Thing To Do; but, easier does not mean easy.

A person may still have to use Courage and Fortitude in order to live with The Correct Decision.

The Wisest of the Wise live their lives on an even higher level than this. They simply avoid having difficult problems.

Therefore, they do not have problems to solve, unless they choose to accept ones not of their own making.

Before I continue, I must return to the sentence "They simply avoid having difficult problems."

This statement does not mean the obvious way to live on a higher plane is to avoid ownership of problems. It means the manner in which people living on This Higher Plane avoid them is "simple" or obvious to them.

They avoid problems because they know how to live "In Accordance with The Way Things Are" All of the time.

There can be no problems if you live This Way.

If you live "In Accordance with The Way Things Are," and you believe there is a problem, you are judging Creation and finding it lacking.

Now, That Is A Problem with No Solution!

Actually, I believe it means the problem is You Are Not Living on the plane you think you are. You still have work to do.

In Zen practice, Satori can be defined either as Total Enlightenment or as a more limited, intuitive understanding of The Way Things Are (a quantum piece of Wisdom granting a "quantum piece of Enlightenment").

I believe the smaller piece of Wisdom is a brief glimpse of This Plane of Being which is in accordance with The Way

Things Truly Are. If you can acquire enough glimpses of This plane, gain enough understanding from This Plane and spend enough time there, you can achieve Self-Realization[2] and full Satori.

Like all true states of being, this one cannot be accessed at will. The work to reach this destination must be done in advance of arrival.

Unfortunately, no one can know the time or place of their arrival at this destination. This forces us to be constantly preparing for our arrival. We must always be Consciously traveling towards that destination. If we let our attention waver for an instant, That Instant might be The Exact Moment when we pass our station by without getting off.

Perhaps we can agree:

"Knowledgeable" means a person possesses more than the average amount of factual information.

"Intelligence" refers to the ability to process factual information leading to the understanding of that information which generates new information and new understandings.

"Wisdom" refers to the ability to put information and understandings in their Proper Place and Proper Prospective in The Way Things Truly Are And act accordingly.

---

2 Self-Realization: As used here by me, refers to the obvious: realizing who and what your True Essence is and its relationship to Everything else in Creation.

A "Few" Words About Enlightenment

I am sure most of us smile.

Of course, it is true some people smile more than others do; some don't smile enough; some people literally beam ear to ear when they smile; and some barely part their lips.

However, none of this is important here.

What is important is the following:

Understanding the process behind the simple act of spontaneously smiling is of great importance to anyone who wishes to Realize his True Self.

OK. Perhaps you are wondering what does smiling have to do with Enlightenment?

Well, now you've got me. Because the answer to this question is:

Not much, if anything, at all.

However, The Process which lets a smile appear on your face without a conscious, preconceived feeling and/or a reaction to that preconceived feeling has Everything to do with Enlightenment.

There have been many times more books and articles written on the subject of Enlightenment than there are people who have attained Enlightenment.

Obviously, another book will not be the answer for everyone.

However, since (almost?) everyone who has ever lived has smiled, everyone has experiential knowledge of one of the key elements of Enlightenment.

This is the reason why I have written this book.

If I can help you realize you already know how to surrender yourself to The Way Things Are by discussing the process of smiling with you, perhaps you can find a way to surrender yourself to The Way Things Are more often.

Many Wise teachers say, in order to reach Enlightenment, we must burn all of our books. They say this even though they continue to write more books all of the time.

In fact, even though I completely agree with them, I have written this book for the same reason they have written theirs.

How can this be?

If what I am saying is true, how can anyone believe I am not writing this book for my own selfish purpose?

Here's the answer:

I feel it is My Duty to share what I have learned.

Although I realize what I have learned is not unique and many books have been written about this same subject, I am doing my best to present this information in a manner I believe will enable some people to begin "To Learn" or experience this information for the first time.

Polishing One's Mirror

Along with realizing and manifesting the process of smiling, there is one more step that must be taken to reach Enlightenment:

We must Purify Our Hearts.

This is both the good news and the bad news.

Why?

Because it is very hard for us to conquer our ego unless we have already been Purifying Our Heart All Along The Way.

In fact, these two processes are almost the same thing.

In Japan, the process of Purifying Your Heart is called Polishing Your Mirror.

If you can watch things unfold exactly as they are Truly unfolding, without adding any personal judgments, coloration and/or assumed history or future, then you are acting like a clear, polished mirror.

If you can't do this; and instead, you add or subtract content, assumed reasons, moral judgments, etc. to or from what is happening, then you are just like a dirty or distorted mirror.

The Spirit of Smiling

You are not reflecting back or sending out exactly what is coming in to you.

You are like a wavy mirror in an amusement park's fun house.

You are changing everything you come into contact with and everything that comes into contact with you. No image in the fun house mirror is an accurate representation of what the real objects look like.

However, if someone did not realize the image in this mirror was a distorted reflection of the actual reality, they would think what they were looking at in the mirror was the only reality.

When this happens even good people with good intentions can make grievous mistakes.

Why?

Because even though they want to think, say and do the right things, they are acting on false information.

Perhaps you are thinking: "Don't I have the right to change things as I see fit" (or see them as I wish them to be)?

I don't know. Do you?

Did anyone give you that right?

Is having the ability to do something, the same thing as having The Right to do it?

I don't think so. What do you believe?

Whether you have the right to change things or not, perhaps the more important question is "Do you think you have the Wisdom to make the Right Choices?"

In this instance, "Right Choices" means those choices which would enable Things to manifest their True Nature.

Does this mean I am saying we should never do anything or change anything?

Absolutely not!

Changing something that needs to be changed is not the same thing as changing something because we cannot understand it for what it really is.

If you think about it, restoring things to The Way They Really Are is actually not changing them into something else. It is restoring them to their *Suchness*: their underlying Reality or Truth.

Let's return to the fun house and take a look at the image in the distorted mirror again.

Kindly notice my choice of words. I did not say let's look at the distorted image again.

Why?

Because I believe if the mirror was reflecting the image back properly, according to the way the mirror's own inherent distortions dictated, then that image was a true image for that mirror.

The distortions were not due to some kind of problem in the atmosphere, the ambient lighting or with our eyes.

The distortion is caused solely by the way the mirror was made.

The Same is True for us.

The distortions that cause us to see Things as different from The Way They Really Are are due solely to the way we are currently made.

We are actually seeing Things exactly as we should be seeing them when you take into account the current defects in our Heart of Hearts, or as some Yogis call it, in The Cave of Our Heart.

Therefore, in order to change The Way we see Things, we need to change ourselves by correcting the defects in our mirror. We can only accomplish this by Purifying our Heart. Then, we would have a much better chance of seeing Things As They Truly Are.

Why haven't I mentioned we see things through our eyes with our brain?

For the simple reason that for all practical purposes, we don't.

OK. I know I seem to be contradicting all the accepted scientific knowledge on the subject of human vision. And perhaps I am. However, the key word here is "scientific."

Sometimes, the scientific process can never seem to grasp "The Way Things Truly Are."

The light which enters our pupils, strikes our retinas and finally travels up our optic nerves as an electrical signal to the vision center in our brain, may actually accurately represent whatever it was that originally reflected that light to our eyes.

However, I believe those electrical signals cannot form themselves into an image that we can actually "see" before what is in Our Heart can transform that image into a reflection of how Our Heart perceives that image to "actually" be.

It is as if the image which begins to "appear" in our brain is instantaneously sent down to our Heart which transforms the image into what It perceives this object to be. Then our Heart instantaneously reflects that changed image back up to our brain's vision center for us "to see."

Our Heart will Add whatever it thinks is missing in the True Reflected Image. Our Heart will also Subtract whatever it thinks should not be in the True Reflected Image. It will continue to do this until the True Reflected Image that came down to Our Heart mirrors exactly what our Heart's preconceived notions about the True Reflected Image are.

Of course by that time, the image we actually "see" is no longer the True Reflected Image.

This is how we are constantly making Our Own Reality.

This process is accomplished so smoothly and quickly "we" don't notice a time lag. We are not normally aware of this process. This is the reason why we believe we are seeing things as they actually are.

As long as we are not aware of this process, we will never attempt to change it. We will remain doomed to act on erroneous information. Information colored by our past experiences.

If a person makes a decision based upon erroneous facts, the only chance he has of being correct is pure random luck.

However, when we can see Things As They Truly Are; then, and only then, is it possible for us to consciously act in accordance with The Way Things Truly Are.

Then, if a person makes a decision based upon knowing exactly How Things Truly Are, there is No Chance the decision will be wrong.

Perhaps you are wondering how I can say that.

After all, isn't there a chance that even if a person is given all of the correct facts, that person can still come to a wrong conclusion?

Yes; if you frame your question like that.

However, framing your question like that ignores the fact that in order to see "Things As They Truly Are," a person must first have a Pure Heart.

Having a Pure Heart is the only way anyone can truly see or realize how "Things Truly Are."

A Pure Heart cannot come to the wrong conclusions if It is processing information based upon how "Things Truly Are."

Why?

Because, once you see "Things as They Truly Are," you will also see how Everything fits together and how Everything actually works.

How Things fit together and how They work cannot be separated from what They Truly Are.

Once You Know All of This, How could you possibly make any other decision except the correct one, The Absolute Only One.

A Pure Heart will not color the value of the choices according to its own value system because it doesn't have its own personal view point.

Therefore, without another set of values to judge things with, A Pure Heart will see only one outcome to enable, which is The Way.

When a person can do this 100% of the time, they will be Enlightened.

Simple is Good, or Is It?

Does this make Self Realization sound too simple?

Sorry; but, it can only be what it is.

Of course, there may be many intermediate steps you must take in order to reach your goal; but, they will all consist of variations and pieces of the two requirements I mentioned above.

Unfortunately, The Path to Enlightenment may be simple; but, that does not mean it is easy.

Indeed, which path would you say is easier?

A long twisting path with many turns offs, forks, steep climbs, sharp slippery descents, rock falls, dangerous animals, hot days, freezing nights and very little water or a straight forward path which is only a tightrope stretched over a narrow, but perilously, deep canyon?

Isn't the one which runs over the deep canyon much simpler?

Yet, I am sure many people would choose the much longer, much more complicated path.

Why?

The Spirit of Smiling

Because in this case, it is obvious the shorter, simpler path is not the easiest one.

Everyone knows there is absolutely no room for error on the high wire. In this instance, this is what makes the simpler path the much more dangerous path, even though the alternative route is no cake walk either.

The simpler path reduces your whole life down to just two things: you and the rope.

In fact, the highest goal to aspire to in order to successfully complete this path would be to reduce your life down to just one thing: You and the rope.

That's correct; it's not a typo.

There are no longer two separate things.

There is no longer a you without the rope. Your whole life would boil down to how well you and the rope can become one thing, one entity.

This kind of one-mindedness and unity does not suit most people.

You cannot stay on the rope and at the same time think about what would happen to you if you fell, if a wind gust blew you off balance, a bird started to fly around you, etc.

You can't even think about keeping your balance on the rope. You must do it without consciously thinking.

There is no time for our conscious mind to consider what is happening or to figure out exactly what must be done and then put that plan into action. In the time it takes to do all of these things, you would have already fallen off the rope.

So what can you do?

Just do the exact right thing every time you have a choice about how to move or not move.

OK. Did you catch me there?

I said the last sentence as I thought you would expect it to be said. However, that is not The Way It Is.

In order for the sentence to read correctly, it would have to be:

Just do what has to be done each and every time something needs to be done.

There should be no choice available. If you are good enough, the only thing that would appear in your mind is the Right Thing. Since only one thing appears, there can be no choice.

Simple, isn't it?

Yes, Absolutely.

Why?

Because All of The Hard Work has already been done.

The Spirit of Smiling

If you did the work to understand the process of walking on that tightrope well enough, then there would be no work left to do.

This is why Enlightenment seems, or is made to seem, very complicated.

People try to find a way around this simplicity because simplicity is much too difficult for most people to understand, let alone accomplish.

I do not have a problem with them trying to take a more complicated approach to reach Enlightenment.

However, I do have a big problem with them making it seem as if the complicated way is the only way to get there. This point of view ignores the fact this is just one way of dealing with something you are not yet prepared to deal with.

Making things complicated is an easy way for us to overlook our shortcomings. This approach is also one of the best ways to insure our eventual failure.

Let's look at another example of why we find it difficult to do something that is simple:

Balancing with only one leg standing on the ground.

Can you do it for 10 seconds? 30 seconds? Even longer?

Do you eventually lose your balance at some point in time and fall?

Why?

I mean if you can do it for 10 seconds, why not forever or at least until your muscles actually give out and stop working, compelling you to collapse onto the floor?

The reason why most of us eventually lose our balance is our mind loses its focus long enough for our body's center of gravity to shift beyond our point of no return.

When that happens, the forces acting on us become so uneven our body is forced by the laws of physics to move in the same direction the greater force is pushing it. Before too long, we lose our balance and fall to that side.

If we were able to keep the forces acting on our body in balance forever, we would stand on one leg forever or until our muscles gave out.

What Really Gets Tired?

No one decides to lose their balance, fall and hurt themselves.

However, just about everyone's mind gets tired of listening to their body's feedback. It becomes bored or tired; or at least that's what our ego wants us to think.

Our ego periodically needs to reassert its control over our thoughts and actions. It accomplishes this by leading our attention away from our balance and towards something of its choosing.

In a sense, we have already lost our balance the instant we stop giving it as much attention as our skill level requires us to do. This is true even though it will take us more time to realize we are "losing" our balance.

How do we "suddenly" realize we are losing our balance if we are focused on something else?

Our instinct for self-preservation will override our ego's demand for control whenever our sub-conscious mind determines we are about to injure ourselves due to a lack of control over our body. Self-preservation will then literally blow our ego into the background.

The Spirit of Smiling

This immediately lets our conscious mind focus on the most important subject at that moment, which in this case, is trying to regain our balance.

We must always remember in order for an ego to be an ego, it must be in control.

Otherwise, our ego is not being an ego. It has no other purpose in its "life"; and, so from its point of view, this is a fight for its survival.

Unfortunately for many of us, our egos can usually win its fight for survival unless it is up against an Immediate threat to our continued existence. I used the word "Immediate" because if the threat is perceived as serious, but the consequences are a long way off, our ego will still win its battle with most of us.

If this was not true, there would be no overweight people and no smokers.

However, this subject can be a whole book, maybe even several books, unto itself. So let's return to examine in more detail what makes us lose our balance.

If our minds wander and we lose our focus, our bodies will shift without our being aware of it. Even though our nerves keep giving us the same feedback at the same "volume," we just stop listening to them because our focus and attention have moved on to something else.

Therefore, I believe what gets tired is actually our Intellect.

It gets tired of trying to assert its control over our ego; especially because our egos are very good at deception.

It is very easy for our ego to make it seem as if our Intellect really hasn't lost its control.

The ego makes it appear to us our Intellect genuinely changed "its mind" simply because it wanted to or our intellect's voluntary relinquishing of its control to the ego will actually result in something more enjoyable than what we are doing now.

The fact that we let our ego get away with its manipulation of our life is a testament to its skill, a statement of how unaware we are of ego, our True Self or both.

Thinking vs. Doing vs. Being

I think I probably need to spend some time demonstrating how we can do what appears to be The Right Thing without first "thinking" about everything that needs to be considered.

OK?

Great!

Then let's consider this example.

It was a favorite of my late Yoga Guru, Yogiraj Swami Bua, Maharaja of Hatha Yoga, whom I refer to as Swami Ji.

If you see your good friend hold up his arm and repeatedly wave it and his hand back towards himself, you will immediately understand he is asking you to walk over to where he is.

You just know it.

You don't think to yourself the following:

"I am seeing my friend's arm moving in a certain way. This means he is calling me to come over to where he is standing. He is my friend, so I will do as he asks.

The best way for me to accomplish this is to walk over to where he is. In order to do that, I need to put my right foot forward first and then my left foot and repeat that until I get there. And all the while I am moving my feet forward, I must make sure to keep my balance so I don't fall over and get hurt."

Yet, every one of these actions (and thoughts) gets accomplished automatically by us. This automation has enabled us to consciously lose track of these kinds of every day processes because they get done at a level below the radar of our consciousness.

Every one of those actions must get done in the proper sequence or we would never reach our friend.

However, instead of thinking about what we are doing at the moment, we are thinking about other things, possibly such as: why is my friend calling me over? I really don't want to be with him now. The last time he called me over, he asked me to do something I really did not want to do. Etc.

We all know this on some level. Yet, as we see our friend wave us over, we are not aware of this concept.

Once we acknowledged our friend's action in our mind and begin to walk towards him, our mind immediately moves on to the next thought and goes somewhere else.

Swami Ji used to say the action was already completed The Instant we acknowledged the arm calling us to come over to that person.

What need is there for us to think about an action that we have already completed?

Absolutely None.

So we are free to think about something else while we are finishing an action which, as far as our mind is concerned, is already completed.

Do you see how this course of action is setting us up for failure?

And, if not for failure, at least for "not as close to perfection as we could achieve" if we applied a little more Intention focused on the action we are doing in Real Time and not on the action happening in our ego's time frame.

This concept of living in the future forms the basis of the old adage:

"A coward dies a thousand times. A brave man dies but once."

Each time the coward thinks about how he may be killed and what it might feel like, he experiences his own death.

The brave man does not follow his future to his own death. He only knows he is alive now and he has something which he has to do at this moment. When the moment of his death arrives, he knows he will deal with it then and not before.

If this fact has been known and acknowledged as true by everyone all through the ages, how is it we ignore this concept in everyday life?

As I said a little earlier, I believe we can ignore this fact because if a person lives only in the present AS IT TRULY IS and does not let his mind wander all over the past and future, he will have effectively taken control of his mind away from his ego.

Our egos will fight us tooth and nail to prevent this from happening. Its most effective weapon is subtlety. Our ego leads our mind away from ourselves to where it wants our mind to go without us even being aware that it has happened. All we usually know is that at some point we realize our mind has wandered away and fixed its attention on something else.

Some people may realize this in one minute or less, while others may take much longer. The longer it takes, the more things can change in that time.

It is like driving a car.

We all blink (close our eyes) all of the time while driving a car and nothing that happens immediately after the blink surprises us. However, if we kept our eyes closed for two minutes and continued driving, we would probably be in big trouble.

The key to staying on the road and having enough time to make all of the right choices is being aware of the present.

When you are driving your car with your eyes open and you begin to approach the street where you live, you will initiate the process of turning the car without consciously thinking about it before the time to the make the car turn arrives. However, if you closed your eyes for a minute and opened them just as you reached your street, you would probably panic as you tried to figure out if you could make the turn at the speed you are going, if you had enough time to hit the brakes in order to slow down enough to make the turn safely or if you needed to by-pass your block and then turn around after you have figured things out.

What is the difference between these two scenarios at the exact moment of having to turn the car?

When you are driving with your eyes open, you are unconsciously, continuously adapting to the changes that are occurring. As you get closer to your turn, you automatically start slowing down to a safe turning speed and begin calculating when to start turning the steering wheel.

If you are driving with your eyes closed and open them just before the turn, you will have no time to adjust to the reality of the present situation. This will cause you to panic and experience unnecessary stresses because you realize you have too much to do in too little time.

Unfortunately, it is very difficult for you to hear or pay attention to what your subconscious mind (I do not like the term unconscious mind because of what it implies) has already figured out because your panic-stricken conscious mind is shouting out nonsense.

Remember, it is a well-documented fact: if our conscious mind is like a computer with limited storage capacity and limited processing speed; our subconscious mind is like a super-computer with virtually (no pun intended) unlimited storage and almost instantaneous processing speed.

I must ask you another question on this subject. It is also one from my Yoga background.

Imagine you are trying to focus on one thing; but somehow your conscious mind slips away and is actually intensely absorbed on focusing entirely on something else.

After some amount of time has passed, you suddenly realize "where" you are. You are not with the object you are supposed to be focusing on.

If you were totally absorbed in focusing on this other subject, "who" made the realization you were somewhere else?

Perhaps I should have asked "what part of you" made this realization.

The answer depends upon whether or not you consider your ego to be a part of you or separate from you; and, whether the "you" I am using here refers to the "every day, normal you" or "The Real You."

Yoga and many other Eastern traditions say everyone has something or someone who is the Ultimate Watcher, the Ultimate Decision Maker.

Unfortunately, this Ultimate Entity (Our True Self) does not like to swim upstream against the current. Our True Self will stay where It is and continue to watch "us" from the background until such time as things are to Its liking.

Then, and only then, will Our True Self make Its move.

We cannot force Our True Self to the forefront by ordering It to "Move It out" or "Shake Its butt." We can only let Our True Self do what It is supposed to do by making the ambient conditions more to Its liking.

Then, and only then, will Our True Self manifest and do what It is supposed to do.

When we let our True Self out of the cage constructed by our egos; and, we think and simultaneously do what we are thinking of, we Will Be what we are doing.

Most people agree we make our own Reality. I want to add a very strange twist to this concept:

Make your own Reality match The Way Things Truly Are by letting yourself become One with Whatever That Reality is.

Therefore, if you are hammering a nail with a hammer; the first thing you need to do is become the hammer. You need to stop "holding it," and just become it.

Of course I do not mean we are supposed to become a physical "hammer." But, if a "hammer" is what we call the object that is best suited to driving a nail into a piece of wood, then we must become that object, and hence, a "hammer."

On the physical level, it is not about becoming the hammer; but, about letting the physical hammer become a part of you. This will require you to let your physical boundaries expand just enough to encompass the hammer.

Next, we need to try to become the nail at the exact instant of contact with the "hammer" (or should I say "with you").

Does this sound insane to you?

OK. But, I did warn you I will be presenting some simple, but "different and difficult" concepts. This just happens to be another one of them.

If you make your own Reality and you can feel your energy move down your own arm to your hand; and, from your hand down to the head of the hammer, you will now be connected to the hammer in the one of the same ways you are connected to your arm (via your Internal Energy, which is called Qi in Chinese or Prana in Sanskrit).

This is not Very easy. It does take some work; but, it is truly easier than it sounds.

The next step is harder.

At the moment of impact, it is possible to feel your energy extend through your arm, into the hammer and into the nail.

And if you drive it home, you can feel the hammer and nail making impact with the wood.

At that point, for the short amount of time your hammer is in contact with the wood, you will be energetically connected to the wood.

You will have expanded your Energetic Boundaries all the way to the wood.

If you can accomplish all or part of this, you will cease thinking about driving a nail into a piece of wood, to actually driving a nail into a piece of wood to finally Being that whole complete process.

There is not a "you," a hammer, a nail and a piece of wood. There is only the process of you driving the nail into the wood.

This is as "In the Moment" as You Can Get.

This is Being.

The Process of Smiling

Now, let's get back to Smiling.

How many of us walk around harboring a moment to moment desire to smile?

How many of us go out of our way to do something that will make us smile simply for the sake of smiling? (Not for the feeling that would accompany the smile)

No one I know of.

Of course, we all do things to make us feel good; and, sometimes that will bring on a smile. However, I believe we do those things to feel good, not to smile solely for the sake of simply smiling.

So, if this is true, why do we smile?

Why not end the process with feeling good?

Is it because smiling is a way of communicating our feelings to others?

If this were true, why do we smile to ourselves when no one is around to see it?

The Spirit of Smiling

Because I truly believe we do not smile a True Smile.

A True Smile Does Us.

(If you are still here, I thank you for your patience. However, I must warn you from here on in, I will be pushing the limits of what most people are used to hearing.)

When we perceive things have changed in a way that pleases us, a smile appears on our face. We do not have to think about smiling once some elusive part of us has decided to let a smile appear on our face.

Indeed, we usually do not even acknowledge to ourselves we are now feeling as if we need to smile.

We just do or experience whatever it is we do or experience just before we smile and feel whatever that action lets us feel. At that point, we just automatically smile along with it.

Think about it.

Is there a point in time when you feel a smile is just about to appear on you face?

Is there a certain feeling you have to consciously acknowledge before you decide to put a smile on your face?

I don't think so.

It seems to me when the conditions are right, a smile will appear on our face without any conscious volition on our part.

We do not weigh the results; and, determine a smile is in order.

We do not smile for someone else.

We do not even smile for ourselves.

We do not seem to smile for any reason other than to smile because the conditions at that particular moment warrant the appearance of a smile.

This process, or lack of a process, means our egos are Not involved with the process of making a True Smile appear on our face.

How About A Little Magic?

In fact, I believe not even our True Self is involved with the making of a True Smile.

There were no decisions made, no feelings acknowledged, no facts deliberated before the True Smile appeared.

To say Our True Self is not involved in the process of letting a True Smile appear on our face is not totally correct.

Our True Self is involved to the extent it notices the process and just lets it happen.

Of course this raises the question: If someone is aware of something and does not do anything about it, is the act of not doing something truly an action or the absence of an action?

I believe if you are aware of something; and, you chose not to interfere with that something as it unfolds, than your choice to do nothing is an action as real as any other.

Therefore, to put it as simply as possible:

When the conditions are Right, a smile appears on our face.

The Spirit of Smiling

Just like that. Like Magic.

Speaking of which, aren't truly special smiles called "Magical"?

Most of us think this is true because "Magical Smiles" make other people smile just by looking at them.

Why do you suppose that is?

I believe it is because when you see that kind of smile, a True Smile, your attention gets grabbed by it. Thus enabling you to forget all the reasons you currently have for not smiling at that particular moment.

So guess what?

If you do Not have a reason not to smile, You Smile!

Is this Magic or is it "The Way Things Should Be"?

Most spiritual traditions describe Enlightenment or Salvation as being a State of Bliss, which is several steps higher than mere Joy.

Delving a little deeper into the act of smiling, we can see as long as a smile is lighting up our face, our ego has disappeared because we are in a non-judgmental moment.

We have surrendered to the smile. And, in the act of surrendering, we enabled the manifestation of what our True Self is experiencing and feeling: Joy or, perhaps even, Bliss.

Most spiritual traditions consider Our True Self or Soul to be Eternal.

Now, hold on to your hats, because I am going to take you on a wild ride again:

When I say something is Eternal, I will mean it is Unchanging. This is what Eternal really means.

If Eternal means it will exist forever, how can it change?

The moment it changes, it, as it was, ceases to be.

Therefore, if our True Self is Eternal, It is Unchanging.

If It is Unchanging, how can It be full of Joy one moment and sad and suffering the next?

I believe It can't.

It is one, the other or perhaps neither. Just whatever it is, It Is….as in "Always Is."

I believe our True Self to be Joyous.

I have no hard proof to offer; only a lot of heavy weight company over thousands of years.

Now, let's take a look at the reverse process.

When the conditions which made us smile change, doesn't our smile disappear immediately?

The Spirit of Smiling

It disappears without our deciding to make it go away.

We don't say to ourselves we wouldn't be caught dead smiling at this new set of circumstances. Or, we must wipe that smile off of our face immediately because something has changed.

How about when the situation hasn't changed; but, our smile somehow automatically starts to fade at some point in time. Who is it that actually judged how long a time our smile should last?

Who timed how long we were smiling?

Did you ever realize: "Oops, I really meant to smile just a little while longer"; and, so made your smile reappear for another 10 seconds?

Or did you ever decide you were not smiling bright enough or perhaps too brightly for a given situation, and made the necessary corrections to your smile?

How is it that Every Smile turns out to be just right?

I believe it is because We don't smile.

So the process is fool proof.

A Smile knows What to do, When to do it and How to do it.

We are the ones who mess things like this up.

So if we take a step back, relinquish control and let a True Smile do what It knows Best, there is No Chance of error.

Gary Giamboi

A True Smile is not human!

Humans may smile; but, if a Smile was human, there would be mistakes.

Since there never are any mistakes with anything about a True Smile, It is obviously not human in nature.

A True Smile is a natural part of The Way Things Are.

No one and nothing interferes with this particular process.

Nothing comes between you and your smile as long as you are smiling.

The instant something does come between you and your smile, your smile disappears; or at least, it changes the way it was.

If you think this is nonsense, then try to force yourself to surrender to a True Smile.

Notice I didn't say "force yourself to smile." I said "surrender to a True Smile."

It has been scientifically proven the very act of smiling can change your mood for the better.

You don't have to think about something to smile about.

Just put a smile on your face and most of the time your mood will brighten for as long as you can keep your ego at bay.

In other words, you mood will lighten until your ego can attach your mind to something other than the smile.

If you can do this long enough and deep enough, you may end up surrendering to the smile and your smile will become a True Smile even though you didn't think there was anything to smile about to begin with.

Or perhaps, this is another instance when the state of our True Self can emerge; because, by temporarily stopping our mind's current processes and focusing our intention and energy on smiling, we temporarily forget we don't have any reasons not to smile.

In any case, it is only important you Surrender to the smile in order to make It True.

This smile will last until your ego re-emerges, takes back its control of you and you finally "remember" you don't have a reason to smile at that moment.

You can easily see how Pure a person's Heart is by noticing what can bring a smile to his face.

For example, if a person smiles because something bad has happened to an enemy, I believe that person's heart still has some black in it.

Another person may smile only when something pleases their senses. While this is not as serious a flaw as the previous issue, it still indicates there is work to be done to that person's heart.

Then again, another person might just take everything in, just as it is, and Smile just because things are The Way That They Are.

No more or less.

This is spontaneous Joy.

This is what we should all be striving for.

But, perhaps you are thinking "What if you take everything in and things are the way that they are; but, they are not The Way They Should Be"?

Jeez, now you went and really did it!

This is the question whose answer has probably killed more people than any other single cause/issue/development in the history of mankind except old age and disease.

If someone perceives things are not The Way They Should Be, then many believe it is their duty to set things right.

The big problem with this course of action is this decision is usually made by most people's egos and not by their True Selves. Hence, the big differences in opinions.

You see, our True Selves, being all the same, would all have to come up with the same answer to the same problem every time.

How Many Different People Are There?

Whoa!

Who said our True Selves were all the same?

OK. Just me (at least in this book).

However, for the moment, let's assume I am mistaken on this point. So just for the moment, let's grant that each person's True Self is different from every other person's True Self.

Now, let's look at a point common to every religion I know of:

Letting God's (or god's) Will be done.

It doesn't matter whether God is actually the Western Judeo-Christian God or another Supreme Entity such as Allah/Buddha/the Dao/etc.

From now on, let's call this set of actions "The Way."

If every spiritual tradition and religion seeks to help us let The Way be done through us; or, at least, not have us thwart The Way; then, if we followed their teachings (which all agree on this point), we should all be doing the same thing given the same set of circumstances.

Why?

Because even God/The Supreme Entity can only have One Will for one set of circumstances (The Way Things Truly Are).

At this point, I must acknowledge the people who always counter logical points about God by saying that God can do anything He wants or be Anything He wants whenever He wants to for as long as He wants to.

To that, I always ask, "How many Eternal, Unchanging Gods are there in Your Creation?

It certainly sounds as if there is more than one, especially if That One is All Knowing, All Wise, All Just, All Perfect, etc.

Now let's ask ourselves: How many All Perfect courses of action can there be?

If One is the Perfect One, how can Another be just as Perfect?

In my book, there can be only One Best course of action, One Perfect Action based upon Perfect Knowledge and Wisdom.

Using a similar train of thought, we can answer the question, "How many different people are there when they will all always do the exact same thing given the same set of circumstances"?

If two people will always do the same thing given the same set of circumstances, are there really two different people?

I say no.

Nobody would be different from any one else if they always did the same thing given the same set of circumstances.

Think about it.

Everyone would always think the same thoughts, say the same things, do the same things, wear the same outfits at the same time, pick the same houses to live in (of course they would all want the same location too), etc.

Now, I know this does not recognize the possibility of different people all doing the same thing for different reasons.

However, from all points of view except a Karmic[3] one, the reason an act is performed makes no appreciable difference to the rest of Creation as long as the act is performed in the exact (as in no difference whatsoever) same way given the exact same set of circumstances.

---

[3] Karmic: As used here by me, refers to the process of the Law of Karma which says that if a person performs an action while being attached to its results, then that person will acquire some quantum amount of pre-disposed tendencies which will cause new defects to The Mirror of Their Hearts. That person will carry this debt and its defects with them until that debt is "paid" by living through some set of circumstances which will "burn ," use up or otherwise repay that debt. Thus, removing the defect from their Heart.

Both Good Karma and Bad Karma produce defects which must be purified before one can reach Enlightenment. Good Karmic Debt can help negate Bad Karmic Debt. However, until a person stops producing Karma of any kind, that person has "Work" to do.

The Spirit of Smiling

Do you remember the beginning of one of the most famous prayers in the Christian world?

"Our Father who are in Heaven,

Hallowed be Your Name;

Your Kingdom Come;

Your Will be Done,

On Earth….."

Just whom do you think is supposed to do "His Will" here on Earth?

You, I and everyone else.

If everyone was doing God's Will and only God's Will all of the time (because let's face it, if God has a plan for humanity, it has to be All Inclusive. There can't be any loose ends unless you think God has gotten a little sloppy in His "old age."), where and when would our egos surface?

What decisions would there be for anyone to make?

What difference would their opinions make?

If a slave always does his master's bidding, is he his own person?

Many people would say, no.

So, if someone with no say in his actions ceases to be his own person if he is always doing another's bidding; then how can someone who voluntarily always does someone else's will be considered a separate person from the one whose will he was always doing?

They can't. (This is the argument fought by feminists and housewives for years).

So even if I am wrong about our True Selves being all the same in theory; in spiritual practice, we are all striving to make them all the same any way!

The only way out of this dilemma is to purify your Heart until no selfish desires remain.

If each of us had no selfish desires and our Hearts were Completely Pure, we would all have the exact same desire(s) given the exact same set of circumstances.

This would lead All of us to "Freely" and automatically think, say or do the Exact same thing at the Exact same time.

Oops, this brought me (us) back to my point of "Sameness" again.

The Process of Letting Things Come to Us

So far, I am sure most of you think all of this seems as if it is an awfully long way from a smile. (Especially considering what expression is most likely on your face at this moment.) But, it is not far off my mark, at least not in theory.

My point about a smile being a spontaneous, non-judgmental, correct action which did not involve the use of our ego is exactly the same process needed for things to happen in accordance with The Way.

We need to step back, become rooted in the present and let things unfold as they should.

Are you ready for another example?

Great, because here it is:

It's the seventh game of the World Series, tie game, ninth inning, two outs, bases loaded, three & two count.

Although the very next pitch and the very next swing of the bat (or lack of) will determine who wins the World Series and who loses it, how can the mechanics of throwing the pitch and swinging the bat, and the decisions which lead to those two actions be any different than those processes are in any other pitcher vs. batter situation where both parties are trying to do their best for their team?

I say Absolutely Nothing is different.

It is just the perception of the outcomes which haven't happened yet that change the moment for the pitcher and batter. The batter and the pitcher tend to get caught up in the outcome (future) of the next pitch and swing and not on just the next pitch and swing.

However much attention they focus on the future is that much less they possess to focus on the present.

Now let's take a look at the slightly less intense process of hitting a major league fastball without the added pressure of winning a game.

This skill is something most of us are familiar with on some level. Most of us have watched it being done at the major league skill level. Almost as many of us have actually swung a bat at a ball pitched to us by one of our peers.

If we look at the hard factual numbers of the speed of a major league fast ball (plus or minus ninety five miles per hour), the distance between the release of the ball from the pitcher's hand and the bat at the point of impact (plus or minus fifty five feet), we get a total travel time of less than four tenths of a second from the time of release to when the bat would make contact with the ball.

In those four tenths of a second, the batter needs to perform everything needed to see the ball, determine if, when and where he should hit the ball and, finally, execute the swing of the bat almost perfectly.

I say almost perfectly because even if the batter's timing is perfect and he makes impact at precisely the right instant, if the height of his bat is off by a few millimeters, he will hit a ground ball or a fly ball; and, if his height is perfect, but his timing is off by a few milliseconds, he will hit a foul ball. So as you can see, even almost perfectly may actually be too imperfect to result in a base hit.

Now, let's make the plausible assumption the ball will travel a certain distance from the pitcher's hand toward the batter before all of the processes which make up the batter's vision finally enable him to see the ball. It turns out that this uses up about one quarter of the fastball's travel time.

Next, the batter has to decide what kind of pitch is coming (fastball, curve ball, etc.) and whether or not the pitch's trajectory warrants him to swing at the pitch.

At this point, if he does decide to swing, the batter must then use his remaining time to calculate the exact point and moment of impact; and, then to figure out how to make his bat arrive at that exact point at that exact moment while traveling at the correct angle.

All of this takes the next two quarters of the ball's travel time.

In the last one quarter of the pitch's travel time, the batter must then give the command to swing and execute the swing according to his calculations.

The Spirit of Smiling

All of this is just not possible using only the processes which occur in the conscious mind. Conscious thinking is much too slow to accommodate split second decisions like these.

The same kind of too short time frames apply to a goalie in ice hockey or soccer having to decide when and where he needs to be in order to prevent the ball or puck from getting past him.

Yet, these people do accomplish these "impossible" tasks.

How do they do it?

There is only one way: sub-consciously.

They must surrender their consciousness and their egos, learn to trust their gut decisions; and, let those decisions manifest themselves without conscious interference.

If we go back to the last inning of the last game of the World Series scenario I described above, and add an ending where the last batter stuck out and lost the game; I am sure we would hear someone say "The batter tried too hard" or "He shouldn't have swung for the fences."

Without knowing it exactly, these people knew the batter's desire to win the game surfaced and interfered with his normal swing process. The batter's desire to win pushed the mechanics of his swing from his subconscious mind into his conscious mind.

Unfortunately for him, his conscious mind was not able to handle the task at hand.

Or how about this example:

During practice rounds, pro-golfers will routinely hit twelve to eighteen inch putts into the cup using just one hand on their putters while they are walking and talking their way off of the green. Yet, once in a while, a Pro will miss one of these putts in a sudden death playoff for a million dollars even though he is thoroughly "concentrating."

How is this possible?

What changed?

Nothing about the putt itself changed.

It was the Pro who changed.

He left the present place, time and putt.

He was in a future time with or without the prize money, or he was "watching" himself being watched by 50 million television viewers around the world and wondering what they would think of her if he missed or made this putt.

So, instead of just putting the golf ball into the hole; he was attempting to make the putt while he was thinking about some other time and/or place. He might have been good enough to do one of those things well. Unfortunately for him, he was simply not good enough to successfully do both at the same time.

So this brings me back to the beginning.

The Spirit of Smiling

The process or lack of a process which brings a smile to our face is something we need to cultivate if we wish to evolve as spiritual beings. The more we can let things do or be us, the less our egos will decide.

The less our egos decide, the greater the chance things will unfold The Way they should.

I'd like to pose one last question on this subject. It is from my Yoga instructor, Yogiraj Swami Bua.

He would ask people: "Do you go to sleep, or does sleep come to you"?

Whenever anyone answered they go to sleep; Swami Ji would immediately ask them to go to sleep then and there.

When they started to "hem and haw" and eventually admitted they couldn't, he always ended up making his point.

He knew they now knew the correct answer. He would end those conversions by saying: "That's all"!

Speaking of sleep, I pray that so far all of my nonsense hasn't let sleep come to you!

What other ramifications can there be in letting things come to us?

There are several possibilities; but, let's focus on just a few for now.

One of the most important concepts to understand is the very act of trying to get something will change you.

Remember my example above of the baseball game? How many times have we said a star athlete was unsuccessful because he was trying too hard to get a hit, throw a strike or hit a long drive?

What exactly does this mean?

Does it mean we should not try to do our best with everything we possibly can? Should we hold something back somehow?

Does the advice to "Relax" mean not try with all of our ability?

I don't think so.

I believe it means to try as hard as you can with all of your ability; but, without becoming attached to the outcome.

Our duty to ourselves and to others is always to do All we can in Everything we do.

It is Not to always be successful

This is not possible.

The outcome of our present efforts is not determined solely by our present efforts.

The Spirit of Smiling

In fact, our present efforts can actually end up being one of the less important factors in determining the present outcome.

What can I possibly mean by this?

Let me answer this with another short story.

Let's say there are two guys in a gym trying to bench press 300 hundred pounds. The first guy hasn't come to the gym very often and didn't put much effort into his training when he did. The second guy consistently trained long and hard.

When it came time to attempt the bench press, the first guy who hadn't trained much knew he was in danger of failing and so he tried to succeed with all of his might. However, due to a lack of training in the past, he failed.

The second, well-trained guy needed just 75% of his strength to succeed. Therefore, he accomplished his goal easily.

Clearly, in this case, the past had more to do with success than the present. If it didn't, then the guy who used 100% of his ability would have won.

Now let's imagine the well-trained guy sent a friend out to buy him some lunch before the event began. He gave his friend strict instructions on what to buy and where to buy it.

However, his friend decided he could spend much less money if he bought inferior items at another restaurant.

Unknowingly, the well trained guy ate the inferior food. His stomach became upset. His illness robbed him of some of his power. At that moment, he could not lift more weight than the first guy, even though the first guy was nowhere near as strong as the second guy would have been if he wasn't ill.

Although we may say perhaps this outcome was the well-trained guy's Karma or Fate, clearly it was something he did not have direct control over once his Karma set things in motion.

In this case, which athlete would you wish to be: the one who won the contest or the one with greater discipline and greater ability?

Obviously in this scenario, the past training efforts of the two weight lifters and their present efforts ended up having less influence on the outcome of this event than other factors beyond their control at that moment.

One of my favorite stories concerning what happens when you try too hard to get something is the following old Zen story.

One day a new student approached his master and asked him:

"Master, if I study very hard every day, how long will it take me to master these subjects"?

His master replied, "Ten years."

The student replied: "That is much too long. I want it much sooner than that. What if I worked twice as hard every day"

Without hesitating, the master replied: "Twenty years"!

What if We Got What We Wanted?

What if we actually end up getting what we desire?

Isn't this what we all truly want?

Maybe. But, here is the Bad News.

Unfortunately, the very act of our actually getting something will change that something into something new. It will change into something that it wasn't before you got it.

Or perhaps even worse, it will change you.

Wait, there's something even worse than this: Both you and it will be changed.

How can I say this?

It is simple, really.

If nothing changed, then you would have had that something before or you still would not have it.

What do I mean by this?

The Spirit of Smiling

If you wanted to catch and own a wild free range mustang because you admired him so much, would he be the same horse once he was no longer free, but owned and controlled by you?

Wouldn't you be changed now that this one desire was fulfilled and it was replaced by a whole new set of desires?

How about desiring to be married to a particular person?

Is either person the same after they are married?

Absolutely not.

They may be better. They may be worse. But, they definitely won't be the exactly the same.

How about a hammer?

If it is owned by a shopkeeper, it is an item to be sold to make him money. If it is owned by a carpenter, it is a tool to work with. If it is owned by a bad person, it may be a lethal weapon to kill someone with.

So which of these very different things is it?

As you can see, it ceased being a just a hammer.

Its purpose became linked to the purpose of the person who owned it.

If you saw it in the hands of each of these different people, you would understand it was something different each time.

Yet, if each one used it for their own purpose, then put it down and left the room so that when you entered the room and saw the hammer lying on the table, you would think it always remained the same and never changed.

So which of the things above was truly the hammer?

Did it remain just a hammer in the hands of each of these people or did it become what the person who controlled it made it do?

Obviously, the Essence of the hammer never changed. However, its purpose became that of its controller.

We are the same way.

Our Essence and Our True Purpose Never Changes; but, our temporary purposes can be those of Our Controller.

To Change or Not To Change?

Sorry, I couldn't resist that. Where was I?……Ah…….

That is correct. We can take on the characteristics and purpose of our controller, our ego.

If that happens, we will become its tool; and, in the eyes of the world, we will seem to be whatever our actions make us seem to be.

But, as powerful as our ego might be, it cannot touch our True Essence, That which makes us our True Selves.

Our life's True and only Real Purpose is to regain control of our True Selves.

And like it or not, Change is the only way to do it.

The question then becomes, what must change?

We can change or everything else can change.

Of course at this moment, our egos are saying "To hell with everything else. I am what I am and I will stay this way"!

The Spirit of Smiling

It is a frightening concept to let "yourself" disappear forever.

Perhaps it is best to avoid the word "forever" and just stick to the here and now, this one moment. This is not so frightening. One step at a time can eventually equal one thousand steps in the same direction and take you to your destination.

Speaking of change, perhaps you are thinking, maybe I don't have to change. Maybe I can change something else instead?

OK. So then, which way is the better way: To be changed yourself or to change that which you are trying to get?

Before, I delve into this question, let me say it is almost always (if not always) easier to change the thing you are trying to get rather than change yourself.

For example, let's say you are trying to learn how to do a complicated physical action for which your body is not strong, fast or coordinated enough for you to do at the present time. You can either work hard at changing your body and mind or you can lessen the demands of the action to the point where you can successfully perform a lesser version of the original action.

The same principles are true for the mental and spiritual goals you set for yourself. It is easier to water down your principles than it is to change yourself too much (or enough).

So what are we to do?

Unfortunately, this is another age old question whose answer is very elusive.

Let me share these thoughts with you:

1) Always Aspire to lofty goals.

One of my favorite quotes is by Michelangelo:

"The great tragedy of life is not that people set their sights too high and fail to achieve their goals, but that they set their sights too low and do."

Why do I chose to use the word aspire?

Because "To Aspire to" is a softer concept than "To Desire," "To Want," "To Pursue," "To Train for," etc.

Always try to move forward to somewhere which seems closer to where your aspiration is. But, always try to tell yourself, you are only practicing or working because it is your duty to practice or work.

You are not working or practicing to actually get something.

However, if while you are practicing, you just happen to begin to become more like what you are aspiring to, Great! Lucky You!

If not, well, so what? You were only doing what you should be doing anyway.

As you can see, this concept involves your very reason for being alive.

We all must decide for ourselves why we think we are here, alive and on this Earth.

Is it for no reason at all?

Is it purely for pleasure?

Or is it for some higher purpose which relegates this life and plane of existence as a mere tool to be used to achieve our Ultimate Purpose?

If you are waiting for me to answer this question for you, I am afraid you will be waiting until I change my mind on what is appropriate for me to do.

I have answered this question for myself; I have not answered it for anyone else; at least, not in this book.

If I start answering these kinds of questions in this book, then the tone and purpose of this book will change.

I do not want it to appear you must accept answers to questions you do not need to accept in order to benefit from the questions and concepts in this book.

I believe the processes I have attempted to describe in this book will work for you regardless of how you answer this question for yourself.

I believe this is an integral part of a concept's Universality and a True measure of its Truth.

Gravity works whether you know how it works or even believe in its existence.

Indeed, as of now, no one knows exactly why or how gravity works. Many people can explain everything else about it. But, they can't explain its Essence.

However, all of us know everything we need to know about in order to know it, live with it and use it in our lives.

The Process of Smiling works the same way.

We may not know everything there is to know about Smiling; but, we can know All we need to know in order to make that process work for us.

2) Do not judge yourself against your aspirations.

Why?

Well, if you have not experienced what you are trying to experience, how can you use that for an accurate reference?

You can't.

You can only use what you think it is like and that is not the same thing.

You are setting yourself up for failure if you judge yourself against what you are not.

3) Do not judge yourself against what you were.

Why?

Because you are no longer that person, so what difference can it make?

You will only become unhappy if you judge the changes to be too small; or you may become too proud of yourself if you see they are great.

There's a good chance you may become too depressed, too eager for more or so self-satisfied you lose your sense of purpose and desire to change.

4) Things will come to you.

What those things will be no one can say for sure.

No one knows well enough the person you were, the person you are now or the person you will become to say for sure.

As you and your circumstances change, new things will look at you and they will decide whether things are just right for them to appear to you, in you, with you and through you.

Every time you perform an action, your body, mind, intellect and ego will change.

This means that you can acquire new physical skills, new mental capabilities, greater will power and concentration.

Or, Unfortunately, you can lose them by the same means.

These changes will allow new and different Spirits to be manifested in and through you.

It could be the Skill of a Great Warrior, the compassion of a Selfless Saint, the Wisdom of a Famous Sage.

Or Not!

The choice is up to you.

If your actions propel you Higher, things on the Higher Planes will be more apt to come to you.

If your actions propel you Lower, things on the Lower Planes will be more apt to come to you.

It is Really that simple.

Remember, this holds true for Every Action.

Not just the ones You think are important.

You can never be sure which action will bring something important to you.

It is just like trying to decide if you should run a stop sign.

During the rush hour when you know an intersection is busy, you will probably decide it is too dangerous to attempt to run a stop sign. Yet, many people do it without getting into an accident.

On the other hand, it could be three am and the streets appear to be completely deserted. So you decide not to stop; and BAM! You get hit.

We all know the only way to make sure we don't cause an accident by running a stop sign is to never run a stop sign.

If we do not Always reach Higher, then perhaps we should remember what "Dirty Harry" said to the bank robber as the robber was deciding whether "Dirty Harry's" gun had one more bullet left or not:

> "You've got to ask yourself one question:
> Do You Feel Lucky"?

Moving Beyond Our Egos

What do I mean when I say "You will begin to resemble The Spirit of these special people"?

By this, I mean you will no longer seem to be like your former self.

You will Act, Feel and/or Think like someone else.

When someone looks into your eyes, they will see a different light burning there. This new light is a reflection of the New Spirit burning within you; and the New Spirit is a result of the New Energy within you.

Traditional Chinese Medicine says a person's "Shen" (their spirit, as in, a spirited race horse) is very dependent on the Qi (energy) of their Liver.

The Liver's element is Wood and Wood fuels your Fire.

Our eyes are the gateway to our Liver.

Therefore, it is in and from Our Eyes that our Shen or Spirit shines outward to the world.

The Spirit of Smiling

What about "Spirit" as in a metaphysical spirit?

Well, if you believe some one's Spirit is Unique, Individual and Eternal, then it is still out there somewhere.

If a Spirit happens to notice there is a living human body which has the same Spirit/Energy of its previous human body, could it not be possible it might decide to drop by for a visit or perhaps even "live" in this new human body for a while?

All individual sources of Energy possess their own particular frequency(ies). They are attracted to or repulsed by the frequency of other energy sources.

This means if you can get the frequency of Your Energy to match that of another source of Energy, the two energies will be drawn to each other. The closer the frequencies match, the greater the transfer of Energy between the two will be.

Energy always naturally flows from the larger source of Energy to the smaller one. More specifically, it flows from the source which exists outside of ourselves to that which is inside of ourselves: From a Great Warrior, Saint or Sage into ourselves.

What if there aren't any unique individual spirits or energy sources?

In other words, there are no unique individual sources of Energy available for us. Instead, there is just one Universal Reservoir.

In this case, the Universal, Uncolored Energy that comes to us would take on the characteristics of the place or person it was residing in.

For example, if you plug a refrigerator into a wall socket, the energy, in this case electricity, would be manifest as coldness. If you plugged a radio into the same socket and the same source of electricity, the energy would manifest as sound.

The reason the same energy manifests itself differently is because the two machines have different operating parameters. One was designed to take away heat, and the other to produce sound.

The same is true of people.

The Energy that enters us will take on the characteristics of our Hearts.

If our Hearts are programmed to value Goodness, the Energy that comes to us will produce Goodness.

If our Heart is programmed to value money, power and fame, the Energy that comes to us may make us ruthless and ambitious in gathering materialistic wealth at the expense of others.

Therefore, if our Heart resembles the Heart of someone who came before us, the Energy that comes to us will produce results similar to those it produced when it came to that other person. We will seem to be like that other person because our Thoughts, Speech and Actions will resemble theirs.

The Spirit of Smiling

And if there is only the One Universal Energy Source, then we will become more like It; and do more of what It would do.

We would start to resemble those who also do (or did) more of what The One Source would do.

What does all of this mean?

I believe it means an ever increasing percentage of your actions will become just like The Act of Smiling.

When the time is right, you will Think, Say and Do just what you are supposed to Think, Say and Do at just the Right moment with just the Right Amount of Intensity for just the Right Amount of Time without even thinking about it.

This means at certain times you will seem to not be "Yourself."

Indeed, your Thoughts, Actions and Words may seem to resemble someone else's.

Remember, for most of us, "Our Self" really means our ego.

So, if your ego has relinquished its control over you to your True Self and you let The Spirit of The Way enter your consciousness, you may resemble someone else who has let the same Spirit enter them also.

Many of us have heard someone say he feels a "Presence." Sometimes he is referring to the Spirit of a particular person (living or not) and sometimes it is just a certain energy which does not seem like his own.

What can this mean?

A person who is sensitive to the energy in his own body, mind and heart will be able to feel the influence of and the interaction of the new energy and his own energy. If he is sensitive enough, he will be able to sense the flavor of the new energy and perhaps even determine its source.

Let me tell you a personal story about this:

Many times over the last twenty four years, I have heard my Japanese Martial Arts Instructor and one of my Spiritual Teachers, Tanemura Soke say "It doesn't matter".

I always knew what the words meant in English.

Sometimes I thought that they were out of place; and, because English was not his native tongue, Tanemura Soke did not mean them totally or exactly as he said them.

I have had a stone statue of a Thai Buddha outside my kitchen window for many years. I always see Him when I sit down to eat.

We have been Good Friends since almost the very first day He came to reside in my garden.

He has a very pleasant face and ALWAYS has a small half smile on it (that's him on the cover of this book).

That's right. He smiles when it is freezing out, sweltering, raining, snowing, day or night. He even smiles when the birds poop on him!

The Spirit of Smiling

I always admired that in him.

Then one nasty, storming day as I was looking at My Friend's smile, I heard the voice of my long time teacher, Tanemura Soke, resonant in my mind with the phrase he often uses: "That's because it doesn't matter."

In that one instant, everything came together for me: the Buddha's smile, Tanemura Soke's words and the unpleasant weather.

I finally realized what Tanemura Soke meant.

Then, I told myself what Swami Bua Ji used to say to me:

"That's All"!

I know this sounds really simple, almost natural.

That's because it truly is really simple and natural.

Let's look at the concept of "Simple" again.

As I demonstrated before, Simple does not mean easy.

In most instances, the simpler something is, the More Difficult it is to perfect.

Why?

Because of the nature of the things which are inherent to the concept of simplicity.

In other words, because of what makes simplicity, simple.

There is No Fluff to hide any errors.

Here is the example I always use:

If you had to bake a strawberry shortcake to serve at a party, it has a high probability of probably turning out good.

Why?

Because, if the cake itself doesn't come out very good, it will be hidden by the strawberries and whipped cream. If the strawberries are not sweet enough, you can soak them in sugar water before you put them on the cake. And, just to make sure the whole thing tastes good, you can always add sugar to the whipped cream.

On top of those tricks, your cake will be served at a party where everyone is already in a good mood and looking at the good side of everything.

On the other hand, if you had to bake a loaf of French or Italian bread for a small diner party, you would have to be spot on.

Why?

Because the only ingredients you can use are flour, yeast, salt and water. You have nothing else to hide your mistakes.

Even the people who have come to the diner party will not be distracted by anything else. They have come solely to eat and enjoy the food without the distractions of a larger party.

So remember, if you hold yourself to high standards, Simple will almost always mean difficult.

Unless of course, you have already done all of the hard work, open yourself up and just smile!

By the way, that reminds me of an old saying in the Martial Arts:

Train Hard, Fight Easy; Train Easy, Fight Hard!

Now that we have established a few of the ground rules, let's take a closer look at one of the most common pitfalls people encounter when they try to surrender themselves to the process of just Being:

Not living in the Present.

This is probably the most common error people make.

Why?

Because our ego usually does not have much control over our present surroundings.

However, it can have complete control over what we chose to remember (the Past) and how we are going to react to it right now (actually, in the very next moment, which is the Future).

This means although it may not be able to completely control the circumstances of our immediate surroundings, it can control how we perceive things.

This is All it needs to control in order to gain effective command over all of our actions.

For example, we can remember the events that led to our last smile and become so engrossed in them that we smile again. This new smile is valid. It's coming into existence can be the result of our having followed all of the correct procedures prior to its appearance on our face.

However, it does not have the same value as it did the first time it appeared because this time, the smile is based upon something that no longer exists.

Its premise is false. So it is false.

The same rules apply to the future.

In other words, if you start thinking about something you believe will happen and those thoughts bring a smile to your face, that smile will also be false because it is based upon something which hasn't happened yet and may never happen.

Does this mean I am saying we must never remember the past or consider the future?

Absolutely Not!

What I am saying is we must always realize that our pleasant memories of the past and our pleasing thoughts about the future are nothing more than Memories and Thoughts.

They are not something we should let ourselves be drawn into in order to experience them again as real. They are not real because they are not in the only reality which should exist for us – The Here and Now.

At any given moment, we can exist fully in only one of these time periods. Therefore, I can make the argument that since All of us is needed to make us as we are, the splitting of ourselves between two time periods ensures we are not ourselves in either.

In order for us to experience our memories and thoughts as real, we must abandon The Here and Now so we can surrender ourselves to our self-manufactured mental circumstances. A pleasant thought about something which does not exist should not become a pleasant feeling or emotion which exists in the present based upon our personal mental constructs which exist in the time period or place we transport ourselves to.

Our True Self can only be Now. That was or will be Then.

We can't work on or affect a change upon a person who is not present!

Being in the past or the future is not being Here and Now.

Many people find the idea of surrendering their egos, their individuality, repulsive and not normal. I agree.

However, that doesn't relieve us of our duty to accomplish this objective.

An easy way to begin this process is to tell yourself you are only going to do it for one moment at a time: only right now, not forever. This is the basis of 'One Day at a Time."

As you become more comfortable with this process, you can connect a few "Nows" together and end up with a longer practice. When you are able to consistently connect together enough "Nows" to create an unbroken sequence of surrender, you will have gone a long way to conquering your ego.

A Little Bit About Free Will

Right about now you may be wondering what your Free Will will be doing while this process of surrendering is occurring.

So let's take a look at some possible scenarios:

First: let's say you don't believe in the reason for not doing what you want to do; but, you force yourself not to do what you want to. This is always the toughest fight to win because you don't believe in the reason you must give up what you desire.

Second: You can see and believe in the reason for sacrificing your desires; but, you still want what you want for your own happiness.

This fight is easier; but, it can still be a tough one to win on your own.

Third: You sincerely want to act in accordance with The Way Things Are more than you want anything else. This decision is easy. There is no struggle.

The Spirit of Smiling

Let's look at the first two scenarios.

The first one, where you do not believe in the reason for doing the action, is by far the most difficult. If you do not believe in what you are doing, the action has to be driven only by your Intellect. Your Heart is somewhere else. Therefore, it is one against one: your Intellect (the challenger) vs. your Ego (the Reigning Champ).

The second scenario can be easier. In this one, your Heart is supporting your Intellect. This fight is two against one: your Heart and Intellect vs. The Champ (your Ego).

However, don't let the numbers fool you. This is usually a battle between two flyweights vs. the Heavyweight Champion of Your World.

The line between the two scenarios can be blurry at times. Your ego will spread misinformation to your heart in order to get your heart to change sides or to sit the battle out; thereby changing the odds back to one on one.

Why? Simply because your ego "understands" that it has a better chance of winning the fight if it doesn't have to fight your Heart also.

For example, how many ways can you think of to justify not giving money to a panhandler?

Whatever that number is and however great the justification for them might seem to be, exactly how much would giving up that 50 cents or one dollar actually affect your life?

Sure, that money may end up being used for a purpose you don't approve of; but, who are we to know that for sure; and to judge it, even if we did know the future?

How many of us think we are too smart to fall for the stories the panhandlers want us to believe?

If we really believe strongly in our own intelligence, why do we have to prove it to ourselves by not helping someone who is in need, even if we know they can survive without our help?

Why do we judge them?

We'll look at this a little more closely in a little bit.

Now, let's return to the first and second scenarios of not doing what you want to do; and add to them peer pressure, other people's opinion of you and/or fear of punishment.

These outside influences may help produce behavior that is considered more acceptable to a society; but, it doesn't help purify the hearts of the people in that society.

We must remember if we consider society to be a living entity, it is more concerned with its own survival than anything else.

Society does not really care whether or not its tools of peer pressure and punishment make you a better person. It only cares its tools make you behave in word and deed like a better person would.

Here is another scenario where the lines get blurred:

The Spirit of Smiling

You still want what you desire; but, what you truly desire is to please someone else out of genuine love for them.

Does this make Your Heart any purer?

In a real way, you would still be doing what you want to the most. Isn't that still selfish?

Perhaps; but, my gut feeling is this action is on a higher plane than acting strictly for yourself.

So what has this to do with our Free Will?

I believe as long as we are pursuing something we desire to make ourselves happy or free of suffering, we are Not using our Free Will.

We are being ruled by our desires for pleasure or avoidance of pain. Using our Intellect to figure out the best way to accomplish this is not the same thing as using our Free Will.

In order to be sure we are really using our Free Will, there has to be something in opposition to "us" that "we" need to overcome. Otherwise, what "Will" is involved in the decision?

Does water need Free Will to flow downhill?

It is in its nature to flow downhill; and, so downhill it flows.

It is our human nature to want pleasure and to avoid pain. Choosing actions which achieve those ends is like water flowing downhill.

Remember, all ancient religious traditions say Only man has Free Will.

Beings on the lower or even higher planes of existence do not possess Free Will.

Beings on the lower planes of existence act according to their baser nature. Their actions seem Evil to us; but, only because we judge them according to our values.

Beings on the higher planes also act according to their nature. However, their planes are purer than ours; and so their actions seem Good to us.

However, neither of them have a choice in the matter.

They can only act according to Their nature.

By using our Free Will to rise above our human nature and act like a Being on a Higher Plane, we are actually working on giving up our Free Will and assuming the nature of a Being on that plane.

If we do this often enough for a long enough period of time, our nature will change to match that of the plane we are spending the most time on.

In other words, once you achieve Union with The Way Things Are, how could you still want to do anything that was not in accordance with That Way?

You can't.

Since there will be no internal opposition to your acting in accordance with The Way Things Are, there is no need for you to use Free Will.

Another way of looking at this is to realize our actions coincide with our feelings. Notice, I did not say "with our thoughts."

Why?

Because our thoughts arise from our feelings and not vice versa.

If we decide to act in accordance with what our Intellect knows is right instead of what our feelings dictate, we are using Free Will.

Of course, the opposite is also true.

If we decide to act in accordance with our feelings and against what we know is Truly The Right Thing to do, our Intellect has made it choice using Free Will.

However, if we purify our Heart (our feelings arise from our Heart) and our Intellect agrees with what our feelings are telling us, what need is there of Free Will?

One of my favorite ancient stories about Free Will and Karma is as follows:

The Vassal and the Murderer

Long ago, the Daimyo (Japanese lord) of a castle needed to get an important message delivered in person to the head prioress of a convent.

The lord chose his oldest vassal to deliver the message because he felt there was a better chance the prioress would let an older man stay the night in the convent's guest quarters instead of sleeping out in the open.

Since the trip to this monastery was a whole day's walk, the old man left early and walked quickly so he could arrive in time for the evening meal.

By the time the sun rose high in the sky, he was hot, sweaty, hungry and tired. So he began to daydream as he walked and paid no attention to his path.

Soon he tripped over a stone in the road and fell down hard. He bruised his face and dirtied his clothes.

As he got up, he felt dizzy; so he sat down on a fallen tree lying off of the side of the road. Once he was seated and his energy started to return, he began to become angry.

The Spirit of Smiling

He couldn't understand why all of this had to happen to him today. He was too old to make this trip which already had made him tired and hungry. He certainly did not deserve to fall down and get bruised and dirty.

In spite of his rising anger, he was still doing his best to accept his fate. Then all of a sudden, he heard a commotion coming from the place on the road where he tripped and fell. Because robbers and cutthroats were known to frequent this forest road, he stayed hidden behind some trees and peered through them to see what was happening.

What he saw astounded him.

Right on the exact spot where he fell was the country's most notorious murderer jumping up and down and shouting with joy. It soon became apparent the reason for his joy was that on the very spot where the old man fell, this ruthless murderer found a diamond ring lying in the dirt.

This was too much for the old man to accept quietly. It pushed him over the edge. He lost his self-control and his temper went with it.

He started to get angry with the gods.

How could they let this happen?

Didn't his good deeds count for more than this man's countless evil deeds? He spent his whole life trying to be a good person and help others in need.

After a while, his anger tired him out and he fell asleep.

In his sleep, the gods sent him a dream:

"When you were born, your Karma was such that at the exact moment you fell, you were destined to be beheaded on that very spot where you fell. But, because you used your Power of Discernment to know Right from Wrong and then used your Free Will to choose to fight your evil tendencies and live a good life, all that was left of your Karma as of today was just enough to cause you to fall and get a little bruised and dirty.

On the other hand, that notorious criminal was destined at his birth to conquer this land and be made a Daimyo on that exact spot where he is jumping up and down. However, because he chose to ignore what his Power of Discernment told him was Right and instead he chose to do what his senses wanted him to do, he lived a life filled with evil. Therefore, all that was left of his Karma as of today was just enough to enable him to find a diamond ring."

The dream ended and the old man woke up feeling at peace with his fate.

Before we end this section, let's get back to the question of judging someone's request for help.

Almost everyone I know Prays to be given something.

The Spirit of Smiling

Whether it is for themselves or not, they are still making a request.

Remember, my mentioning how easy it is to justify refusing a panhandler's request for money?

Well, according to my way of thinking, associating our prayers to our refusal of a panhandler goes like this:

If the Entity we were making the request of, judged us as harshly as some of us would judge the panhandler, what would be the chance of us getting our request?

Let's be real.

No matter what, because of how we live Our lives, wouldn't almost All of us need to be cut some slack by The All-Knowing and All-Just in order to even be considered "eligible" for being granted a boon?

What chance do we have of "getting over" an All-Knowing being?

None.

Yet, we all try to do that every time we try to convince The All-Knowing of the righteousness of our plea.

Why should we expect to receive more than we are willing to give?

Would You Like Some Bliss?

It is important to recognize the whole process of conquering your ego is The Path to Enlightenment, which is supposed to result in our being in a State of Bliss.

Bliss is actually a very interesting word.

Webster's dictionary defines "Happiness" with words like "pleasure" and "joy." These are two words very much in tune with our everyday world.

The word "Ecstasy" is a step above "Happiness." The definition of "Ecstasy" adds the word "overpowering" to "pleasure" and "joy."

"Bliss," however, stands by itself.

It is The Gold Standard.

It gets the words "Great" and even "Spiritual" added to its meaning.

The Spirit of Smiling

First, let me say I believe the oldest Spiritual Traditions were realized and developed at a time when man was much closer to his True Self, his Spirit and the Spirit of the Universe.

There was much less distraction in his life. He carried around with him far fewer "things" which seemed as important to him as so many of the things we carry around seem to us.

Man Felt more and thought less.

Things were less complicated.

Time moved according to The Laws of the Universe and not according to the whims of man.

Man did not affect the Universe at all. Instead, the Universe affected man much, much more than It does today.

Here's another way of looking at this concept:

At the dawn of time, Man did not think he was quite as important to The Scheme Of Things as he thinks of himself today.

The Bottom Line:

The oldest spiritual traditions come from a time when we weren't so important.

They come from a time when the only Spiritual Ritual was living in accordance with The Way of the Universe.

In the beginning, there was no need for any rituals besides that of living correctly.

Why?

Because living in the world was not separated from the Spiritual part of ourselves or The Universe. The need for religions and their spiritual rituals developed only when man separated himself, his life and the world he lived in from The Universal Way.

Once this separation of Our Being from Creation occurred, mankind decided it needed to devote some quantum amount of separate time, which was not spent as we actually lived our lives, to what mankind decided was The Spiritual Part of The Way.

If not simultaneously to the development of a separate Spiritual Time, then at least soon after, I believe the concept of a separate Spiritual Place came into being.

This Spiritual Place was considered "the best place" to spend one's Spiritual Time.

How sad.

Yet, most people do not even know how much or even what they have lost by segregating their lives into Quantum pieces of existence.

Unfortunately, our modern society with all of its distractions has made it very difficult for people to become aware of the extent of their loss; and, even harder to care about it.

The Spirit of Smiling

The simple fact of the matter is instead of creating a special time and place to be Spiritual, this concept ended up enabling the rest of Creation to become the time and place when and where we Didn't have to be Spiritual.

Although humans can be very stupid, we are not dumb.

I am sure it didn't take us very long to realize that if something required only one or, at best, a few hours of work per week to be performed in a special place, then that one item couldn't be All That Important to The Scheme Of Things.

This realization has evolved into The Human Condition as we live it now.

The most ancient traditions are a way to get in touch with All we have lost.

They are a way to become whole again. They can remove us from The Present Human Condition and put us squarely right back into The Way Things Are.

All religions have the same goal:

To unite Their People, Their Believers to Their version of God or The Supreme in some way.

However, it is Their way of uniting things which tend to be different.

Some religions believe we will be at His feet, some have as existing alongside Him, some believe we will become like Him and some believe we will literally become One or United with Him.

For the purpose of this discussion, the differences in the end result are not important. What is important is this overlooked fact:

In order to reach the end result of All religions, we must stop acting independently.

Instead, they All say we must do God's Will, Allah's Will, Act in Harmony with The Dao, Develop a Buddha Nature, Perform our Dharma according to Sanatana Dharma, etc.

In which of these processes would we do that which we as an individual human being would normally do before we reached these elevated states of being?

None I know of.

So if we are not doing what we would normally do, are we still ourselves?

Have we changed?

It is the duty of every person to decide for themselves what changes need to be made.

In order to do that correctly, we must mature Spiritually.

Just like a child cannot be trusted to make the right choices for himself, a spiritually immature person cannot be trusted either. We must grow and use that new wisdom to make the right choices in order to keep growing and making more right choices until there are no choices left.

In the end, there will only be choices with One Option, which, of course, is no choice at all!

When Is Our Free Will Truly Free?

When do you think your Free Will is Truly Free?

For example: as adults, how many of us use our Free Will in the process of choosing not to have sexual relations with our parents?

I believe many people will answer "All normal people."

I say Absolutely Not One Normal Person!

Why do I believe that?

Because I realize the act of having sexual relations with one's parent does not even present itself as a choice for most of us. We are conditioned to not even consider such things.

Therefore, there was no decision involved. Not making a decision precludes using your Free Will.

I am sure you can think of many more examples of theoretical choices you could make if they ever did present themselves. But, since they just don't come up, you don't make them.

The Spirit of Smiling

If you don't have to make any choices and/or decisions, your path is easy to follow. Just follow Your Nature and take the One "Choice" it makes available to you.

Can you see that following Your Nature does not require Free Will?

Free Will only comes into play when you have an option to Not Be Yourself, to Not Be True to Your Nature.

Where does this leave us?

Guess?

If there are no choices, how could Life be anything but Simple!

This is The Way It Should Be.

How do I know?

What else in the Universe has to really think about what to do in a given situation?

Does water have to think about which way to flow?

How does electricity know which way leads to the ground?

If you drop something, which way does it always fall?

Everything has its own Nature and acts accordingly.

Only those creatures with Free Will can try to go against the Natural Order of the Universe.

Does a tree have a hard time being a tree?

How about a dog being a dog?

Or a cat being a cat?

No, not that I know of.

Only humans appear to have a problem with being human.

Why?

Because Only humans possess two natures.

Even beings from the other planes of existence seem to have no difficulty in being what they are and acting according to their true natures all of the time.

Demons and devils seem to relish being demons and devils. It is what they are all the way down to their very inner most essence.

Angels, Saints, Buddhas, etc. have no difficulty in acting their part because They Are Their Part. It is not an act. They have no conflicting spirits or desires within them.

Only humans possess two conflicting spirits: one is bound to the Earth and the other one is bound to Heaven; or one to a Lower Plane of Being and one to a Higher Plane.

This is why all the religions and spiritual paths I know of say Only man has Free Will.

The Spirit of Smiling

Only man has to choose between two different natures.

Therefore, he is the only one who has to make a choice.

All other beings only act according to their inherent nature which is in accordance with their spirit and their desires.

Until we decide which Plane we want to belong to, we will always be conflicted and torn between the two.

Notice I did not say "until we chose the Higher Plane."

Why?

Because we can choose either one; whichever one we feel more comfortable with.

There is no Right or Wrong here.

There only is Whichever choice is correct for you at that point in Space and Time.

Of course, I believe the Higher Plane is our ultimate destiny; but, perhaps just not here and now for some of us.

This is the Ultimate choice for our Free Will.

It seems to me in order to become our True Selves, we must Freely give up Free Will.

Why?

If the decisions our Free Will makes are based largely upon our impressions of what we have already experienced, our factual knowledge, our ability to understand that knowledge and our present desires, just exactly how Free is it?

Some experts believe if they knew absolutely everything about someone, they could predict exactly what that person would choose to do in every situation.

Doesn't that make us prisoners of our past life (lives)?

Let's take a look at Free Will and Self-Change.

Remember, it can be easier to change the whole world, than to change ourselves.

How can we start this process of change?

First, you must make a conscious effort to be conscious—all of the time.

Do nothing from habit.

Do nothing from the past.

Do nothing in the future.

Develop the Power of Discernment.

Use your Intellect more.

The Spirit of Smiling

Learn to look at, weigh and decide what it is you must do because it is most closely aligned with **What is The Right Thing to Do based Upon The Way Things Truly Are.**

You must be Aware and in the present moment in order to be able to do this.

Another way to help yourself become able to See and Do The Right Thing is to change yourself by picking a habit of yours you don't particularly like and then breaking it.

Why am a suggesting picking a habit?

Well, let's look at what most of us mean when we think about a habit.

It is some kind of action (thought, speech or action) which happens when a particular set of circumstances triggers its manifestation without conscious thought on our part; and hence, when you are not in control of yourself.

Remember what we say about our habits:

- "I can't change it."
- "It is too strong."
- "I didn't even realize I was doing it."

Clearly our habits control us. We do not control them.
Wait! Hold on!

Didn't you just explain that is exactly what a smile does?

Yes and No.

The "Yes" part is they both appear without conscious thought.

The "No" part is the fact the smile is not, or should not be, brought up from our memory. That would not be a True Smile.

However, a habit is brought up from our memory. By its very definition it must be because a habit cannot be a first time spontaneous development.

It may appear to manifest spontaneously. But, it is actually the result of many repeated manifestations. So many that the process gets put on autopilot requiring no conscious thought to make it happen.

After the "why" of breaking a habit comes the "how."

First, you must become aware of when you are doing it; when it is in control of you.

You must notice which circumstances trigger that behavior pattern, that habit. Once you can see what triggers it, you can try and stop that behavior from arising when you see those circumstances developing.

You must pick a small habit to start with. If you pick a big one, it will be like going to a gym and deciding you are going to lift 200kg on the first day.

You need to be real. Start small and succeed.

The Spirit of Smiling

If you keep trying to change your habits, your skill and Will Power will grow just as surely as your strength will grow if you continue to go to the gym.

Eventually, you can overcome even the most deeply ingrained habits.

If you change enough habits, you will cease to be the person you seemed to be.

If these changes result in a Pure Heart, you will become the person you truly are, always were and always will be.

Remember, the greater the number of things which can "Do You" or use you to manifest themselves just as they are according to Their True Nature, the less of "you" that will be interacting with Creation.

This means your ego is becoming weaker and smaller. It is dissolving. This process allows the Real You to begin appearing and interacting with Creation directly. Your Personal Footprint on Creation is becoming smaller.

This process enables you to begin to use the information (knowledge) from your past without coloring it; without using all the coloration you previously associated with it. (We'll look at this subject in more depth at the end of the next section)

Then Everything you do will be done with The Spirit of Smiling.

All of Your Actions will be The Right Action at The Right Time with just The Right Amount of Intensity.

I wouldn't be surprised if this State of Being resulted in your Smiling a whole lot more of the time!

Why not?

You would get to watch yourself perform in the only True "Reality Show" there is. It would be on 24/7 with no repeats, no scripts and definitely no commercials.

So, here we are almost at the end of this "talk," and I did not really explained to you exactly how to accomplish any of this.

Why Haven't I?

Simply because I can't.

I believe no one can.

Why?

Let me explain to you what I mean using these stories:

We are all familiar with the fairy tale wizards who need to speak their spells of power using an arcane language which contains words and names of power.

Without the correct words said with the exact pronunciation and intonation, the spells of power won't work.

In many religions, it is forbidden or considered to be impossible to know the True Name of the Supreme Entity of that religion for several reasons.

The Spirit of Smiling

First, it is impossible for a human to know and understand such a Being or Concept using only human concepts.

Second, knowing this Name would give us power over It, which is another impossibility.

What all of this means is that the True Name of something would contain and thus reveal that thing's Exact and Complete True Nature and Essence.

Thus, the knowing of something's True name would grant us control over that thing.

Therefore, even if the exact mechanism and timing of the processes to achieve this knowledge were known by someone, no known language has the words to express them.

If they did, you and I would be following them at this very moment!

However, this does not mean this knowledge is unknowable.

It is only unknowable on human terms.

In order to understand this knowledge, we need to use methods not associated with our humanness (our minds) and begin to use methods which are associated with the Higher Planes of Existence: Experiential and Just Knowing or Intuition.

No culture I know of has ever associated Goodness with The Below.

We must Rise Above our Lower Nature.

In order to do that, we must travel from within ourselves by rising up with our own Internal Energy.

If you are just about to ask "How do I rise Above with my Internal Energy"; I have to ask you, "How do you not"?

Why?

Because left to itself with No Interference from you, your Internal Energy will rise up by Its Very Nature. All you must do is to: Do Nothing.

See how I keep repeating myself?

I told you in the very beginning of this book, that is what I do because the Principles I work with:

Do Not Change—Ever.

To make the point clearer:

In order to enable ourselves to Rise Up, we must learn to Strengthen our Free Will to the point it can ensure we will do Nothing.

We must let The Right Things Do Us.

The Big Problem with Being Mindful: How Do We Use the Information Stored in Our Memories Without Living in the Past?

This seems to be one of the most frustrating questions students of the Eastern Philosophies have to face.

Given that we are supposed to live our lives only in the present moment, how are we supposed to live a normal life and not be forced to constantly relearn every piece of knowledge we have already learned, if we cannot draw from the knowledge we acquired in the past?

Everyone who is trying to be Mindful and live only in the Now has to answer this question for themselves.

However, I believe that this is not a difficult question to answer. We just need to sit back and look at some of the concepts I have previously discussed.

The Spirit of Smiling

All we must do is examine which part of our memories or knowledge we are supposed to leave in the past because it belongs in the past, and which part of our knowledge is Unchanging and thus is not relegated to only the past.

We are not supposed to leave Uncolored Knowledge in the past.

For example, fire is fire.

Its nature always was, is and always will be fire.

If we remember it is hot to the touch, we will not be constantly burning ourselves each time we encounter fire.

However, if we place our own associations on to the nature of fire in a way that we cannot separate our associations from that of fire's True Nature, then we have changed what the nature of fire is for us.

Let's imagine we were once Severely burned by fire at some point in the past; and, every time we have encountered fire since then, we are afraid we will be burned just as badly again.

In this example, every time we call up our knowledge of fire, we are calling up our past emotional baggage, not just fire's True Nature.

This is not living in the present.

Any decisions we would make would have at least some of their basis in a past which no longer exists.

However, if we were able to recall just fire's True Nature (that it is hot and can burn us if we do not respect it), then we would not be calling up the past because fire's True Nature has not changed.

We could then make our choices based upon Only Upon what is in the present moment without bringing in any of the colorations from our past.

Here is another of my favorite ancient stories. It illustrates very nicely my point about remembering what happened in the past without attaching excess baggage to it.

Two Traveling Monks

An important message had to be delivered from one monastery to another monastery. Since it was a long overnight journey, the head abbot chose two monks in order to help ensure their safety.

He gave the command of the trip to the older, wiser and more experienced monk; and made the younger one his subordinate.

They left at sunrise to make sure they would spend just one night out in the open.

They liked each other; and their skills complimented each other's, so the journey began well.

By mid-morning, their road was traveling beside a swiftly flowing river. They were enjoying the sun, the gentle breeze and the sound of the flowing water, when all of a sudden they heard a woman's frantic calls for help.

The older monk was the first to realize the woman was in the river. So he reached the river's bank before the younger monk.

He saw the woman was drowning and was just about to be pulled into the river's swift flowing center current. He knew he had to act immediately if he was going to save her life.

The Spirit of Smiling

So, he immediately kicked off his sandals and dived in to the river. He reached her just in time and pulled her from the river to safety.

Then, to ensure her as much comfort as possible, he continued to carry her short distance away from the water and laid her down on a patch of grass.

Thankfully, she was unharmed.

As soon as she got her breath back, she thanked the monk profusely.

She explained to the monks her village was nearby; and she was the daughter of the village's chief. She told them not only her father, but the whole village would want to thank them for their kindness.

She offered to take both of them back to her village for a feast in their honor.

They politely refused; explaining they were in a hurry and had to be on their way.

Even though the sun was still shining, the breeze was still blowing and the water was still flowing, the older monk realized the journey had changed. The younger monk had a frown upon his face and was in a dour mood.

The older monk knew the reason for this change and decided to wait until the younger one worked out the problem for himself.

The rest of the morning passed in silence. They also ate their noontime meal in silence. Then, the long afternoon passed in silence; and soon, they were sitting down eating their evening meal in silence.

At this point the older monk lost confidence in the younger monk resolving his problem by himself; so, he broke the ice by asking his companion the reason for his anger.

In response, the younger monk flew into a self-righteous rage:

"How could you touch that woman? We have all taken vows never so much as to even touch a woman with our fingers and you actually carried that woman for a few minutes with her body touching yours. I will never be able to obey your commands again. You are not my superior"!

The older monk calmly looked him in the eye and said: "Yes, I carried a dying woman to safety. I put her down as soon as possible; and, I left her there many hours ago."

"You have never put her down. You are still carrying her around in Your Heart.

Which One of us has more blame"?

One Last Question

Let's assume it was a matter of Your Life and Death you arrive at a particular location for a Life Saving medical procedure before it was too late (and by the way, there was absolutely no way you could be sure when "too late" will be); and, the only mode of travel you had to get there was a very peculiar car.

This particular car had a broken fuel gauge and a fuel tank with an unknown quantity of gasoline in it. It also had a broken, inoperable, unfixable gas cap which was frozen shut, thus rendering the refueling of that car impossible.

Under these circumstances, what would you do?

Since the car could run out of gasoline at any moment and you would not be able to refill the gas tank, how much time would you waste by:

- idling the engine
- making unnecessary stops
- taking "fun" side trips
- carrying extra, unneeded baggage with you which would add to the car's weight and decrease its fuel mileage?

If your answer is: Since your life depended upon arriving before it was too late, you would not waste any of your time doing any of these things with a car that could run out of gas at any moment.

Instead, you would drive as directly as possible to your most important destination.

If this is so, why do you suppose most people live their lives like they will never run out of gas when their life is just like this scenario?

So, if I assume you do not know when your life will run out of time or energy; and, you have no means of replenishing your supply of either, I would like you to ask yourself:

How much of your finite supply of Internal Energy do you waste each day by:

- Thinking wrong thoughts,
- Saying unnecessary words,
- Doing unnecessary things
- Carrying unnecessary emotional baggage?

"Unnecessary" includes anything that does not move you closer to your ultimate destination, Enlightenment.
I know we don't think about it; but, everything, as in Everything, we do consumes some of our life force.

This is one reason the Ancient Yogis, Buddhists and Daoists all practiced techniques to slow down their breathing.

Yes, this is correct. Even breathing uses up some of our finite supply of Internal Energy.

More importantly, breathing at a stronger, quicker pace will speed up our metabolism; which will burn up our supply of Internal Energy at a quicker pace.

If I may return to the car analogy again, if the body we possess was made with a life span of only so many "miles," the faster our metabolism runs, the quicker we will travel that limited number of miles (even if we seem to be going nowhere).

Therefore, to be blunter, even our breathing is killing us.

The taking of fewer breaths conserves your Internal Energy and prolongs your life.

Another interesting fact is that for the most part, the faster we breathe, the faster our mind jumps around.

If you want to calm your mind, one of the easiest ways to accomplish this is to slow your breathing down.

This is another reason why I frequently tell my students most of what I teach them is what not to do, what to let go of. Many times I am also including their breathing in their "Not To Do List."

They must learn to let their mind and emotions let go of their breathing; and just let it happen naturally.

The same applies to all of us.

In order to become Our True Selves, we must let go of everything else, especially our egos.

The Spirit of Smiling

We must surrender and let things come to us in their True Form, with their True Spirit.

In other words, in exactly the same way we don't interfere with a Smile appearing on our face.

If it seems as if I just denied the concept of Free Will, you may rest assured I didn't (almost).

Instead, I have attempted to show how at the end of the processes I have described here; Free Will is what we will use in order not to use anything at all.

Why did I use the word "almost" just above?

Because Free Will is what we use whenever we decide to choose between our two natures.

If there is no need for us to make that choice because we only have One Nature and Our Spirit and Desires are already aligned with It, then there is no choice to make.

If there is no choice to make, there is no need to use our Free Will.

Clearly, I did not deny its existence.

I only tried to show it should be rendered unnecessary, as unnecessary to our lives as it is to Smiling.

That's right.

There is no Free Will involved with the process of a True Smile appearing on our faces.

We are not involved in this process at all.

This is The Way It Should Be.

This is The Way All Things Should Be.

In Conclusion

As you can see, this whole book boils down to

"Do Less, Be More."

The less we add or subtract to The Way, the more we will be acting in accordance with The Way.

The more we act in accordance with The Way, the Closer we are to Enlightenment.

The closer we are to Enlightenment, the More we will Smile.

Or is it: the More we Smile; the Closer we are to Enlightenment?

About the Author

Gary Giamboi was born in the Year of the Metal Rabbit (1951) in New York, USA.

He attended a Catholic grammar school with the Sisters of Mercy, a Catholic high school with the Jesuits and finally Stevens Institute of Technology, where he obtained a Bachelors of Engineering Degree.

He began training in the Eastern Arts in 1969.

The following are the rankings and titles he has received along the way:

- *Kyoshi* (Teaching Master) *and Shibu-Cho* (Regional Director) in the Genbukan World Ninpo Bugei Federation
- *Ryokudan* (6th Degree Black Belt) in the Genbukan World Ninpo Bugei Federation
- *Ryokudan* in the Kokusai Jujutsu Renmei
- *Okuden Menkyo* (equivalent to about a 7th Degree Black Belt) in Asayama Ichiden Ryu Taijutsu in the Genbukan World Ninpo Bugei Federation
- *Chuden Menkyo* (equivalent to about a 5th Degree Black Belt) in Blkenjutsu in the Genbukan World Ninpo Bugei Federation

- *Shoden Menkyo* (equivalent to about a 3rd Degree Black Belt) in Bojutsu in the Genbukan World Ninpo Bugei Federation
- *Nidan* (2nd Dgree Black belt) in Hanbo Jutsu in the Genbukan World Ninpo Bugei Federation
- *Shoden Menkyo* in Gyokko Ryu in the Genbukan World Ninpo Bugei Federation
- *Shoden Menkyo* in Shinden Fudo Ryu in the Genbukan World Ninpo Bugei Federation
- *Shoden Menkyo* in Shinden Tartara Ryu in the Genbukan World Ninpo Bugei Federation
- *Shoden Menkyo* in Gikan Ryu Koppo Jutsu in the Genbukan World Ninpo Bugei Federation
- *Menkyo Kaiden* (Mastership) in Taijiquan and Qigong in the Taishan Guangdong Chen Wei Gun Wushu Federation
- Level 4 (Master Level) in Qigong from the National Qigong Association of the United States
- Level 1 instructor of I Liq Chuan
- Recognized by Yogiraj Swami Bua Ji as an instructor of his system of Hatha Yoga and Hindu Wrestling Exercises including Indian clubs and Rope Yoga. Upon initiation as a disciple on January 17, 2001, Swamiji named me *Gajendranathan* or King of the Elephants.
- E-500RYT Yoga instructor from the Yoga Alliance
- Level 2 instructor in Thai Yoga from Jonas Westring
- Certified Practitioner of Ohashiatsu (Shiatsu) from the Oshashi Institute
- National Academy of Sports Medicine Certified Personal Trainer
- Pilates Mat and Reformer instructor certified by June Kahn
- *Nidan* (2nd Degree Black Belt) in Goshin Jutsu from Sensei Robert Hansen

- Ist Degree Black Belt in Tae Kwon Do from grandmaster Suh Chong Kang

His personal life has been almost as varied as his training.

He started as a "water boy" in the summer of his thirteenth year. He eventually became president of his family's construction company in 1991. Under his presidency, the company did over $200,000,000 in business until it went broke in 2003 due to not receiving payment on several large projects.

In those years, he amassed a small personal fortune; and, at the end, he lost everything except himself, his wife, his instructors, his knowledge and his way in life.

As president of his family's company, he had the final say in what the company did. Therefore, when his father, acting as a partner, could not convince him to sell everything he owned in order to put that money into their faltering company, he refused. He knew the family could get out of the business with both honor and money.

However, his father then decided to "play dirty." He asked Gary again to sell everything; this time as his father and not as a business partner.

Gary did not hesitate. As a son, he agreed to do as his father asked even though he knew the odds of a successful outcome were not good.

He could refuse to act on a shareholder and partner's bad advice. He could not refuse his father any material thing he asked of him.

The final outcome of this decision enabled him to learn the skills of letting things go and living in the present.

To contact Gary Giamboi or to see more of his works, kindly visit:

- www.TheInstituteofAsianArts.com

- http://www.facebook.com/gary.giamboi

- @DharmaWarrior on Twitter

www.ingramcontent.com/pod-product-compliance
Lightning Source LLC
LaVergne TN
LVHW051120080426
835510LV00018B/2136